KATHERINE MANSFIELD'S NEW ZEALAND STORIES

KATHERINE MURPHY DICKSON

University Press of America, Inc.
Lanham • New York • Oxford

Copyright © 1998
University Press of America,® Inc.
4720 Boston Way
Lanham, Maryland 20706

12 Hid's Copse Rd.
Cummor Hill, Oxford OX2 9JJ

Library of Congress Cataloging-in-Publication Data

Dickson, Katherine Murphy.
Katherine Mansfield's New Zealand stories / Katherine Murphy
Dickson.
p.   cm.
Includes bibliographical references and index.
1. Mansfield, Katherine, 1888-1923—Knowledge—New Zealand.
2. Women and literature—New Zealand—History—20 century. 3.
New Zealand—In literature.   I. Title.
PR9639.3.M258Z6353 1998 823'.912—dc21   98-10528CIP

ISBN 0-7618-1072-2 (cloth: alk. ppr.)

♾™ The paper used in this publication meet the minimum
requirements of American National Standard for information
Sciences—Permanence of Paper for Printed Library Materials,
ANSI Z39.48—1984

DEDICATION

To the memory of Paul and the journey never taken

Contents

Foreword

In recent years, interest in Katherine Mansfield's New Zealand stories, which include such individually celebrated works as "The Garden Party" and "At the Bay," has risen precipitously. First published together in 1974, the stories attracted critical remark as exempla of a peculiarly Modernist sensibility: de-centered, female, colonial, proto-postcolonial. Written from within the metropolis, England, yet set in the colonial world of Mansfield's birth and youth, the stories of the Burnells and the Sheridans have seemed to many readers almost definitory, not only of Modernism, but of modernity itself. For central to our century seems a sense of exclusion, of being knocked off-center. And what clearer way to express this sense than in the dialectic of relation between colony and metropolis? The metropolis defines the culture of the colonies from afar, even when one is situated within the de-centered colonial world. Indeed, the metropolis may seem more real in its absence, as a thing longed for or rebelled against, than it later becomes to someone subsequently living within it, and who comes to take it for granted. Logical, thus, that once one is in the metropolis, memory should return to a time and place when the very absence of this defining culture had made it seem more substantial.

Logical, too, that this should be so important among Modernism's repertory for expressing displacement, along with its attempt to give voice to the position of the female, that excluded Other within the domestic world. Romanticism, the forebear of Modernism, situated its own lost world of its poetic imagination in far more unattainable places than in the geographically displaced world of the colonies: in youth, in a more exotic Other world that could never be reached, in the imagination. Modernism, developed in the world of machines and fast ships soon to be replaced by jet airplanes, had to find more mundane contrasts, more real definitions of limitation within the world to express its lingering sense of being no longer at ease. Hence the large contribution made to the literature of Modernism by works written from the perspective of the geographical "outside": Joyce's Ulysses, set in the self-consciously provincial city of Dublin, remains the most celebrated; Eliot, it seems, could hardly have written as he did of the "unreal city" of London had he not, originally, hailed from St. Louis.

In the present work, Katherine Dickson enters the colonial world of genteel, proto-English New Zealand evoked from Mansfield's memory, a world of the far-off and yet so-near. She considers it as a world of contradictions, a world of disjunction on all fronts. There is a marked split visible between the inside and the outsides of characters, leading to estrangement between adults as well as to alienation between children and the adult world. Many of the characters in these stories exhibit a marked fear of death. A strong contrast between dark and light imagery implies a greater gamut of emotional possibilities than most people usually describe, as well as a life more focused on the emotional extremes.

Gender too, the givens of the female experience, as Dickson implies, may have overlapped with geographical displacement to give Mansfield's New Zealand fiction its particular quality. For Dickson is clear that the complexity of authorship, a mixture of qualities of the individual artist as well as the facts of her geographical situation, influences, and gender, resists reductionistic treatment. Dickson concentrates instead on the works themselves, even while pointing towards the questions her analysis raises. The result is a sober and at the same time illuminating reading of some of the central works of what may still be an under-appreciated, if major, twentieth-century author.

> Bruce E. Fleming, Professor
> United States Naval Academy
> Annapolis, Maryland
> November, 1997

Preface

The first four chapters of this book were substantially written as my 1958 master's thesis at Columbia University. Since then, I have read those biographies and critical works on Katherine Mansfield which happened to come to my attention. University Press of America's suggestion that I update my work, resulted in, first, a systematic review of the burgeoning published literature on Mansfield, then, the development of Chapter five of this book. Since the first four chapters are primarily textual analysis, time has not altered my approach. What has changed is the availability of recent criticism by feminist scholars such Susan Gubar, Sydney Janet Kaplan, and Patricia Moran. It is hoped that this book will serve both as an introduction to Mansfield's New Zealand stories, and as an indication of Mansfield's increasing importance as a short story writer and her position as a major figure in British Modernism.

Acknowledgments

Grateful acknowledgment is made to the following for permission to quote previously published material:

From *The Letters Of Katherine Mansfield*, edited by John Middleton Murry, special one volume edition. Copyright c 1932 by Alfred A. Knopf Inc. Reprinted by permission of the Society of Authors, Ltd.

From *Stories* by Katherine Mansfield, selected and with an introduction by Elizabeth Bowen. Copyright c 1956 by Alfred A. Knopf Inc. Reprinted by permission of the publisher.

From *Katherine Mansfield and the Search for Truth* by David Daiches in *The Novel And The Modern World* by David Daiches. Copyright c 1939 by University of Chicago Press. Reprinted by permission of University of Chicago Press.

Introduction

ℰᎧᏩᏑ

In her *Journal* for January 22, 1916, Katherine Mansfield wrote about New Zealand and her work:

> Only the form that I would choose has changed utterly. I feel no longer concerned with the same appearance of things. The people who lived or whom I wished to bring into my stories don't interest me any more. The plots of my stories leave me perfectly cold. Granted that these people exist and all the differences, complexities and resolutions are true to them—why should *I* write about them? They are not near me. All the false threads that bound me to them are cut away quite.

> Now—now I want to write recollections of my own country. Yes, I want to write about my own country till I simply exhaust my store. . . . Oh, I want for one moment to make our undiscovered country leap into the eyes of the Old World. . . . It must take the breath. . . . But all must be told with a sense of mystery, a radiance, an afterglow . . . perhaps not in poetry. Nor perhaps in prose. Almost certainly in a kind of *special* prose. . . . That' s all, no novels, no problem stories, nothing that is not simple, open.[1]

What had caused this statement of new purpose? Several things had, but the most immediate one was the despair she felt over her brother's death in World War I. This had turned her thoughts back to the distant dominion where she was born on October 14, 1888, and which she left, never to return, in 1908. Her homeland, which she had rejected as a provincial wasteland, obsessed her imagination as disillusion with Europe, which had once appealed to her as a cultural mecca, increased in the face of World War I and little literary success.[2]

The first fruit of her efforts to write about New Zealand was "The Aloe," begun in February 1916 and finished as "Prelude" in the Spring of 1917.[3] In this story as in all of her New Zealand stories there is a sharp dichotomy between Beauty and Death and the resultant conflict raises the question of which of the two is real in the duality. The diversity between the two was apparently produced by two separate writing motives:

> I've two "kick offs" in the writing game. ONE is joy—real joy—the thing that made me write when we lived at Pauline; and that sort of writing I could only do in just that state of being, in some perfectly blissful way AT PEACE. Then something delicate and lovely seems to open before my eyes, like a flower without thought of a frost or a cold breath, knowing that all about it is warm and tender and "ready," and THAT I try, ever so humbly, to express.

> The other "kick off" is my old original one, and had I not known love, it would have been my all. Not hate or destruction (both are beneath contempt as real motives) but an extremely deep sense of hopelessness, of everything doomed to disaster, almost willfully, stupidly, like the almond tree and "pas de nougat pour le noel."[4] There! As I took out a cigarette paper I got it exactly—A CRY AGAINST CORRUPTION— there is ABSOLUTELY the nail on the head. Not a protest—a cry . And I mean corruption in the widest sense of the word, of course.[5]

"Pauline" was the villa in Bandol, France, where she had begun "The Aloe," the first story written from both "kick offs." The New Zealand stories investigate the inconsistency between Beauty and Death and work out a synthesis between them. The whole problem of reality in this duality and method of presentation are inextricably linked.

Discarding conventional plot structure, Katherine Mansfield began her stories in *medias res* and usually ended before the climax, because she felt that the introduction and nearly concluded ending conveyed an artificial or distorted sense of life. To penetrate the exterior of conventional behavior and present inner experience, she relied on the dramatic monologue technique. This enabled her with great economy to present various time levels through the daydream and formal flashback. Objectivity or truth was always her aim. "At the end *truth* is the only thing *worth having*."[6] To present the greatest "truth" of an object or character, it must be recreated not just discoursed upon. The author becomes the object in a momentary vision:

> When I write about ducks I swear that I am a white duck. . . . Then follows the moment when you are *more* duck, *more* apple, or *more* Natasha than any of these objects could ever possibly be, and so you create them anew.[7]

About writing "The Stranger" she wrote: "It isn't as though one sits and watches the spectacle. That would be thrilling enough, God knows. But one is the spectacle for a time."[8] And about writing "The Voyage" she wrote: "It wasn't a memory or a real experience. It was a kind of *possession*.[9]

But the universality or truth which she wished to convey must be done indirectly. Speaking of the "tragic knowledge" gained by the experience of World War I, she wrote in a letter to John Middleton Murry:

> But, of course, you don' t imagine I mean by this knowledge let-us-eat-and-drinkism. No, I mean "deserts of vast eternity." But the difference is I couldn't tell anybody *bang out* about those deserts: they are my secret. I might write about a boy eating strawberries or a woman combing her hair on a windy morning, and that is the only way I can ever mention them. But they *must* be there.[10]

To present truth obliquely was her greatest problem: "But how are we going to convey these overtones, half tones, quarter tones, these hesitations, doubts, beginnings, if we go at them *directly*?[11] The tangential approach to her material allowed for the maximum of implication. William York Tindall likened her method to that of the symbolist poets: "She often worked by indirection, allowing overtones, hints, and silences to suggest more than the situation seems to hold."[12] By repeatedly focusing on a minute detail, ostensibly trivial emotion or fragmentary occurrence, she was able by suggestion to work out to some intensity of feeling or universality of meaning about the major forces of life. David Daiches analyzes her method:

She starts with one particular, and such universal aspects as there are emerge very indirectly, by implication, as a result of her organization of detail. . . . Initial observation provided the story—without self-consciousness she observed with clarity, because there was no subsequent process of comparison and reflection to refine and correct the original observation. In this type of literature it is the actual form of the story which gives symbolic (universal) value to the incidents. There is no simple relation between form and content, no story x presented through medium y. The nature of the medium reflects back on, and to a large extent determines, the nature of the content. It is like lyric poetry, a type of writing where conception unites instantaneously subject (matter) with style (form).[13]

Not only did Katherine Mansfield use an oblique approach to her material in building up intensity to the significant point she wished to convey, but because the story ends just before the climax, the climax takes place within the reader. In this way demand was put upon the imagination or poetry-making faculty of the reader. This was in keeping with her desire to convey a sense of "mystery" or a sense of possibilities beyond what is actually stated.

The New Zealand stories were written within a short period of time. "Sun and Moon" was written in February 1918; "The Stranger" was written in November 1920. But the year 1921 produced "The Voyage," "At the Bay," "The Garden Party," and "The Doll's House." The unfinished story, "Six Years After," was written in the fall of 1922, a few months before her death on January 9, 1923. The New Zealand stories, unfortunately, had never been separately published until 1974 by Longman as *Undiscovered Country: The New Zealand Stories of Katherine Mansfield*, edited by Ian A. Gordon.[14] They lay imbedded in the total body of her 73 finished stories and 15 unfinished stories which she wrote before the New Zealand stories from her old original "kick off," or on contract with various periodicals during the time she wrote the New Zealand stories. Because all criticism unanimously acclaim the New Zealand stories as her best work, I think they warrant the study given them in this book.[15]

Notes

1. Katherine Mansfield, *Journal*, edited by John Middleton Murry, definitive edition, London, 1954, pp. 94-95.
2. Up to this time the only book which Katherine Mansfield had had published was *In a German Pension*, London, 1911.
3. See Sylvia Berkman's study of the differences between "The Aloe" and "Prelude" in *Katherine Mansfield, a Critical Study*, New Haven, 1951, pp. 83-102.
4. Katherine Mansfield, *Letters*, edited by John Middleton Murry, special one volume edition, New York, 1932, p. 106. Note supplied by the editor: "This (sic) a reference to a beautiful poem in Provencal by Henri Fabre, the naturalist, telling of the withering of the almond blossom by the cold."
5. Ibid. Feb. 3, 1918, p. 106.
6. *Journal*, p. 185
7. *Letters*, Oct 11, 1917, p. 74.
8. Ibid., Nov. 3, 1920, p. 347.
9. Ibid., Mar. 13, 1922, p. 454.
10. Ibid., Nov. 16, 1919, p. 255.
11. Ibid., Jun. 24, 1922, p. 476.
12. William York Tindall, *Forces in Modern British Literature 1855-1956*, New York, 1956, p. 207.
13. David Daiches, *The Novel and the Modern World*, Chicago, 1937, pp. 75-76.
14. Several early stories contain characters that foreshadow characters that appear in the later New Zealand stories: "New Dresses" (1910), "A Birthday" (1911), "The Little Girl" (1912). Three other New Zealand stories—"Woman at the Store" (1911), "Ole Underwood" (1912), and "Millie" (1913)—deal with murder, insanity, and isolation in New Zealand. For a discussion of these early stories see Berkman, pp. 39-48.
15. After *In A German Pension* (see note 2), *Bliss and Other Stories* was published in 1920 and *The Garden Party and other Stories* in 1922, both by Constable. *The Doves' Nest and Other Stories* was published posthumously in 1923 by Constable. In 1924 *Something Childish and Other Stories*, an assortment of stories of various dates, was published by Constable. In 1941 the collected *Short Stories* was published by Knopf, and in 1956 *Selected Stories* was published by Vintage. This latter work contains stories from all periods of Katherine Mansfield's writing career. These various editions of her work follow a chronological order and therefore the sequence formed by the New Zealand stories is obscured, if not totally lost sight of.

Chapter I

ℬ)(ℛ

The Isolated Outer Person

Communication

In a discussion of the view of reality afforded by Katherine Mansfield's New Zealand short stories it is necessary at the outset to examine the relationships between the characters in the objective world. Only by doing this is it possible to see the inter-relationships between the character in the objective world and the character in his private, subjective world. Perhaps the most significant fact about the view of reality afforded by Katherine Mansfield's New Zealand short stories is that the characters are isolated from each other.[1] Although the characters are presented in the setting of family relationships, the husband-wife and parent-child relationships provide little opportunity for communication and understanding. In fact, communication or conversation between characters is in the nature of an intrusion or interruption. In "Prelude," Linda Burnell is awakened by her husband Stanley rattling the window blind, and she unhappily realizes that her dream about herself as a young girl with her father has been destroyed by Stanley letting in the sun.[2] Stanley interrupts and distracts her musings several times as he briskly gets dressed for work—first explaining what a good bargain he got in the new house and then expressing his fear of getting fat. Linda gives feigned attention until she pleasantly realizes that he has finally gone for the day and will no longer disturb her (p. 67). In "At the Bay," Stanley, himself, has a similar experience of being distracted by conversation when, after thinking that he has the ocean to himself for his early swim, he is rudely awakened to the fact that he is not alone. His brother-in-law, Jonathan Trout, is also in the water and tries to talk until Stanley, not being able to put up with it any longer, tells Jonathan that he is in a hurry and cannot be bothered (p. 103). Perhaps Linda is the one most distracted by conversation, because she gets it both from Stanley and the children. When Kezia, in "Prelude," asks her mother what the strange looking plant growing in front of the house is, Linda answers the child curtly. But after the child's second question as to whether the aloe ever blooms, Linda says that it does bloom every hundred years and then closes her eyes to the child, whose questions disturb the mother's pre-occupation with private feelings (p. 75). These private desires to reject her children are made explicit later in the evening when Linda again stands before the aloe with her mother (p. 92).

Not only is there a failure of communication when one character directly confronts another, there is a deeper lack of communication which amount to a kind of perpetual estrangement between characters. This is the outstanding quality of the husband-wife relationship. Stanley Burnell is so non-plussed by Linda that he explicitly asks her periodically if anything is wrong. He so persistently demands approval and assurance that everything is "all right," that if his wife's attention strays from him he fears he has offended her or that she isn't agreeing with him. On his journey home from the office, in "Prelude," he is overtaken by a panic of fear and is gripped by the idea that something might have happened in his absence (p. 77). After finding that everything is fine, his sudden elation is dashed to nothing when he realizes that Linda is not as glad to see him as he would like her to be (p. 78). Both Linda and Stanley have very sudden changes of feeling but their feelings never coincide.[3] Because Linda smiles to herself when Stanley shows her the new gloves he has bought himself, he asks her if she thinks he was silly and then asks her outright what she is smiling at ("At the Bay", p. 133). Stanley so lacks subtlety that he asks literal questions and expects literal answers. But Linda gives him her usual Mona Lisa smile which completely disconcerts Stanley. Not knowing his wife well enough, nor being able to tell from the context of the conversation what her reactions might be, he is thoroughly distraught. Although he does question her in desperation, the questions are usually irrelevant to his main concern. He asks Linda if she thinks his buying the gloves is silly when it might be more to the point it if he asked her whether she thinks he is silly in general. He poses little literal questions but is never able to articulate his real concern or his real feelings. Although Stanley is unperceptive about his wife, the situation is complicated by the fact that Linda does hide something from him. She has feelings of secret hostility towards him and because of this she tends to withdraw from any encounter in which she might manifest these feelings. There are times when Linda thinks she might disclose to Stanley the fact that she hates him and that she thinks motherhood is killing her. But her motive is not that this disclosure might increase understanding between them, it is rather one of spite. She would like to surprise him and see his reaction. Standing before the aloe with her mother, Linda imagines Stanley a dog:

> If only he wouldn't jump at her so, and bark so loudly, and watch her with such eager, loving eyes. He was too strong for her; she had always hated things that rush at her, from a child. There were times when he was frightening—really frightening. When she just had not screamed at the top of her voice: "You are killing me." And at those times she had longed to say the most coarse, hateful things....
>
> "You know I'm very delicate. You know as well as I do that my heart is affected, and the doctor has told you I may die at any moment. I have had three great lumps of children already. . . ."
>
> Yes, yes, it was true. Linda snatched her hand from her mother's arm. For all her love and respect and admiration she hated him. ("Prelude", p. 93.)

Not only are Linda and Stanley estranged in this way, but all of the wives and husbands in Katherine Mansfield's stories are similarly out of touch with each other.[4] The entire story, "The Stranger," is concerned with John and Janey Hammond's total inability to express their feelings and make relevant responses to each other. In John' s mind, the moment of being alone with his wife, after her absence of ten months, has been built up as a long awaited expectation of fulfillment. After several delays and interruptions—the delay of the boat, Janey's goodbyes, the dealings with the hotel manager and porters—they are finally alone. But Janey is so preoccupied that she hardly notices John. She repeatedly asks for the children's letters, asks about the luggage and comments on the dressing table. John's exasperation mounts until he asks her to tell him that she is really glad to be back. It never occurs to him that she might have a reason for being so distant. He has had a number of hints: he knows the boat was delayed because of a death on board, he knows Janey is dressed in black, he knows she made a great point of saying goodbye to the ship's doctor. He fails to see any significance in these things and is aware only of the fact that Janey eludes a direct confrontation with him:

> But just as when he embraced her he felt she would fly away, so Hammond never knew for dead certain that she was as glad as he was. How could he know? Would he always have this craving—this pang like hunger, somehow, to make Janey so much a part of him that there wasn't any of her to escape? He wanted to blot out everybody, everything. He wished he'd turned off the light. That might have brought her nearer. And now those letters from the children rustled in her blouse. He could have chucked them into the fire. ("The Stranger," p. 237.)

John and Janey are at an emotional dead end; and, in addition to being unable to communicate with each other, they work at cross purposes so that, like Linda and Stanley, their feelings never coincide. They relate to each other in a way that is mutually painful. Both John and Stanley are driven by a love which is blind, which fills the world of each one to the exclusion of everything else. In their fierce desire to totally possess the objects of their affection, they see their wives only in relation to themselves and not as separate persons. Their love is destructive to the relationship. Both Linda and Janey withdraw from what seems to them an assault and this complicates the feeling of estrangement. John Hammond cannot bear the fact that his wife has shared in an experience from which he is left out. Death has come between them in more than one way and John, like Stanley, is consigned to a world he cannot understand.

Not only are husbands and wives isolated and unable to communicate, but parents and children are also estranged. The parents, by failing to respond to the children, reject then and withhold love from them. Linda not only has secret feelings of hostility towards her husband, she is also a reluctant mother, whose children bear the brunt of her feelings. Her characteristic gesture towards her children is that of closing her eyes. In "Prelude," Lottie and Kezia are left behind at the old house because there is only room for the "absolute necessities" in Linda's carriage.

From the carriage Linda looks at the children standing on the lawn and imagines that she is casting them off. She leans back, closes her eyes and smiles (p. 53). Later in the new house, when Lottie and Kezia arrive, Linda asks vaguely if the children have come but she doesn't open her eyes to look (p. 60). The next morning, when the children are out playing, the grandmother suggests that Linda take a look out at her children, but the grandmother says she knows that Linda won't do this (p. 72). When Linda does go out and meets Kezia at the aloe, she is distant and formal in answering the child's questions as has been pointed out earlier in this paper. She smiles to herself and closes her eyes. The children, particularly Kezia, are aware of being rejected. In "At the Bay," after being frightened by the dark and what they imagine to be a spider fallen from the ceiling of the wash-house where they have been playing, the children think:

> Oh, those grown-ups, laughing and snug, sitting in the lamplight, drinking out of cups! They'd forgotten about them. No not really forgotten. That was what their smile meant. They had decided to leave them there all by themselves. ("At the Bay," p. 127.)

This sense of being left out by the adults parallels the experience of Kezia being frightened in the old house after being left alone there ("Prelude," p. 56). Since Kezia is most aware of this feeling of loss of love, she suffers from nightmares in which animals rush at her and camels have enormous, swelling heads ("Prelude," p. 58). She is plagued by something she calls "IT" which hides in passageways waiting to dart out at her ("Prelude," p. 56). The child is afraid of the dark, likes to sleep in her grandmother's bed and asks for a candle at bedtime ("Prelude," p. 62). For the children, only love casts out fear.[5] Because Linda ignores the children, Kezia looks to her grandmother for love. In her estimation of the situation, Linda feels that she doesn't have the strength to love her children, but then she decides, she wouldn't love them anyway.

> She was broken, made weak, her courage was gone, through childbearing. And what made it doubly hard to bear was, she did not love her children. It was useless pretending. Even if she had had the strength she never could have nursed and played with the little girls. No, it was as though a cold breath had chilled her through and through on each of those awful journeys she had no warmth left to give them. ("At the Bay," p. 116).

Mrs. Sheridan in "The Garden Party," like Linda Burnell in many ways, also rejects her children. But she does so when it is to her own advantage, as when she is asked directions about the marquee. Not wanting to be bothered, she tells the children that the party is up to them and that she is to be treated like an honored guest (p. 285). After the accident in which a man is killed, Laura goes up to ask her mother if the party should be postponed. Laura is more disturbed by her mother's attitude than her actual reply. After making sure that the accident had not occurred in her own garden, Mrs. Sheridan doesn't take the situation seriously. She smiles and is amused at Laura (p. 294). Then she "pops" a hat on Laura's head in an effort to distract Laura's attention from the accident (p. 295). While Mrs. Sheridan explicitly states that the children are to be in charge of the party, she indirectly interferes and has things her own way. She distracts Laura's attention from the death by the hat and later, when Laura has forgotten about the death, she decides that it would be a "brilliant idea" for Laura to take the party left-overs to the widow and children (p. 297). Mrs. Sheridan has turned the situation to her own ends without any consideration of Laura as a person.

The father in "Sun and Moon" ignores, or perhaps does not try to discover, what makes Sun so unhappy when he sees the ice house melted and the party decorations spoiled. To the sobs of the child, the father commands: "This moment. Off you go" ("Sun and Moon," p. 195). These stories present a world where communication between people is absent or at most destructive when it does exist. Not only are those characters who share intimate relationships and who live in a situation ordinarily conducive to the maximum in communication isolated but all of the other less closely related people live in a world of isolation.

Perception

Linked with the problem of communication between people is the whole question of perception. The stories present a reality within which failure to perceive another self objectively is perhaps the reason for the lack of communication and love. Perhaps the least perceptive person is Stanley (and his counterparts, John Hammond and the husband simply called "Daddy" in the unfinished piece "Six Years After"). While he is outwardly the model of good sense, he is actually almost pathologically unperceptive. He expects that everyone thinks exactly as he does. In

"Prelude," the first morning in the new house, he joyously exults in the beautiful weather, his own physical vigor and the new house; and he thinks that Linda feels the same way he does. He goes on talking to Linda as he gets ready for work and is oblivious to the fact that she is barely paying any attention to him. He tells her that his friends are getting fat but that he never will as though this were something she should be intensely interested in, but she is far away from him in her own thoughts and just waiting for him to leave. The first morning in the new house is important to Stanley's sense of success and he, quite in keeping with his joy at such a good bargain, exudes self-satisfaction. The first morning for Linda is horrible; she immediately thinks of escaping in a carriage and not even turning her head to wave goodbye (p. 66).

Stanley is constantly rebuffed by the realization that other people, as well as Linda, do not share his ideas about things. He must believe that he is right and that his point of view is right. This admits of no other possible point of view. Consequently any difference to Stanley is a reflection on the rightness of his own point of view. This is disastrous to his sense of well-being, but the shattering experience never leads to any understanding of the other person. He goes from one shattering experience to another, unable to understand why he is rebuffed. The husband in "Six Years After" exhibits a similar lack of perception. He takes his wife up on the cold deck where he would like to be during the journey although he knows she would rather stay in the warm cabin:

But he had come to believe that it really was easier for her to make these sacrifices than it was for him. Take their present case, for instance. If he had gone down to the cabin with her he would have been miserable the whole time and he couldn't help showing it. At any rate she would have found out. Whereas having made up her mind to fall in with his ideas, he would have betted anybody she would even go so far as to enjoy the experience. Not because she was without personality of her own. Good Lord! She was absolutely brimming with it. But because . . . but here his thoughts always stopped. Here they always felt the need of a cigar, as it were. And, looking at the cigar tip, his fine blue eyes narrowed. It was a law of marriage he supposed. . . . All the same he always felt guilty when he asked these sacrifices of her. That was what the quick pressure meant. His being said to her being: "You do understand, don't you?" and there was an answering tremor of her fingers, "I understand" ("Six Years After," p. 344).

Beryl, too; is guilty of projection and attributes false motives to other people. Her whole picture of what the servant girl Alice is like is distorted. In "At the Bay," Beryl, sitting in the window drying her hair, sees Alice leave on her free afternoon:

> She supposed Alice had picked up some horrible common larrikin and they'd go off into the bush together. Pity to make herself so conspicuous; they'd have to work hard to hide Alice with that rigout (p. 121).

But in reality, Alice, who doesn't like to feel "common" and who tries very hard to be respectable, has been invited out to tea.

Indirect Relationships

Not only do the characters fail to communicate, lack perception in regard to each other, and attribute false motives, they also make what might be called irrelevant responses to people in the objective world. The objective world is negligible for these people. In "At the Bay," Stanley has a series of experiences which build up his sense of irritation until finally, when he is ready to leave for work, he punishes Linda by not saying goodbye to her. He not only punishes her for something she is unaware of, but he punishes her not for one thing, but for the accumulation of his feelings of irritation from a series of incidents. First, his swim had been spoiled by the presence of Jonathan, then Beryl had neglected to put sugar in his breakfast tea, then he cannot locate his hat and walking stick; but worst of all nobody seems concerned about his not being able to find his things. He presumes that Alice poked the fire with his stick. As he dashes around looking, he is angered by Linda's lack of concern in the hunt. Linda then becomes the object of his rage and he punishes her by not saying good bye to her (p. 106). But as soon as he leaves the house, he is overcome by a sense of guilt and the feelings he had previously vented on his family now turn inward and become tortuous self-punishment. The whole day is so terrible for him that he finally reaches a saturation point of self-inflicted suffering and for compensation buys himself the pair of gloves discussed previously. He can't wait to get home to beg Linda's forgiveness for his not saying goodbye and to tell her how he has suffered all day because of his neglect. But Linda, when asked for forgiveness, doesn't have the faintest idea what Stanley is talking about. She had not even noticed that he had neglected to say goodbye. The fact that she hadn't noticed hurts Stanley again. He cannot believe that Linda had not realized what he did (pp. 132-133). This kind of confused response, in which the character thinks he is responding to something in the objective world when in reality he is only responding to his own emotions, is common to nearly all of the characters in Katherine Mansfield's New Zealand short stories. The relationships which these people have in the objective world are either distorted or completely one-sided. People like Linda and Stanley carry on what passes for a conversation, though each character has a different and sometimes opposed version of what is taking place. Quite frequently, what appears to be a confrontation of two characters is really a situation in which the second character is just an object or locus for the release of the pent-up emotion of the first character.

Such a situation is illustrated in Beryl's shooing away the Kelvey children in "The Doll's House." What has provoked her wrath is less that the Burnell children are disobeying the order not to play with the washerwoman's children, than that Beryl has had a bad afternoon.

A letter had come from Willie Brent, a terrifying, threatening letter, saying if she did not meet him that evening in Pulman's Bush, he'd come to the front door and ask the reason why! But now that she had frightened those little rats of Kelveys and given Kezia a good scolding, her heart felt lighter. That ghastly pressure was gone. She went back to the house humming ("The Doll's House," p. 325).

Notes

1. Many critics have noted the isolation of characters and lack of contact between them. On this point Desmond MacCarthy remarked in a review of *Bliss and Other Stories* by Katherine Mansfield, in *New Statesman and Nation*, XVI, 450 (January 15, 1921):

> She continues to emphasize what is the distinctive note in her sense of the world—that each person lives to himself or herself alone.

Antony Alpers says in *Katherine Mansfield: A Biography*, New York, 1953, p. 298:

> It seems to have been Desmond MacCarthy who first observed that most of Katherine Mansfield's characters seem to be out of contact with one another—isolated, each inside its bubble. . . .

In an essay on Colette, Louise Bogan in *Selected Criticism: Poetry, Prose*, New York, 1955, p. 30, criticizes Katherine Mansfield for her failure to grapple with the problem of human relationships:

> The stories of Katherine Mansfield, so obviously influenced by Colette, illustrate the Frenchwoman's method of attack without giving a hint of her quality. For Katherine Mansfield's talent leaves off where Colette's begins. The Englishwoman's sensibilities could touch nostalgia, pity, and regret. They could not seek out the difficult human relationship, grasp it in essentials, reduce it to form. Where Colette struggles with the problem on its own terms, Katherine Mansfield shied away.

It was Katherine Mansfield's belief that a story which worked out a "problem" between two people was too specific, too finite. She worked to convey universality of experience, and therefore, a "problem" was much too limited. In a letter to the Honorable Dorothy Brett, written November 11, 1921 (*Letters*, p. 416), Katherine Mansfield states her case:

> Chekhov *said* over and over again, he protested, he begged, that he had no problem. In fact, you know, he thought it was his weakness as an artist. It worried him, but he always said the same. No problem. And when you come to think of it, what was Chaucer's problem or Shakespeare's? The "problem"

is the invention of the nineteenth century. The artist takes a *long look* at life. He says softly, "So this is what life is, is it?" And he proceeds to express that. All the rest he leaves.

On November 26, 1921, Katherine Mansfield wrote in her *Journal* (p. 273) more about her belief that the artist does not work out "problems":

> Reality cannot become the idea, the dream; and it is not the business of the artist to grind an axe, to try to impose his vision of life upon the existing world. Art is not an attempt of the artist to reconcile existence with his vision: it is an attempt of the artist to create his own world *in* this world. That which suggest the subject to the artist is the *unlikeness* to what we accept as reality. We single out—we bring into the light—we put up higher.

It seems to me that while it is necessary to examine the relationships between the characters to understand the world in which they live, it is also necessary to keep in mind that Katherine Mansfield did not intend to write stories which primarily dealt with the everyday problems of human relationships.

The whole question of the characters being out of contact with and isolated from each other brings in the question of the deep-rooted sense of exile in the colonial experience. V. S. Pritchett in "Minor Masterpieces," *New Statesman and Nation*, XXXI, 87 (February 2, 1946), compares "At the Bay" with Chekhov's "The Steppe" and points out the isolation in the former story:

> But in Chekhov we find an indispensable element which is strong in his writing but weak in hers: the sense of a country, a place; the sense of the unseen characters, the anonymous people, what we may call "the others" from which the people of his stories are taken. Katherine Mansfield's "At the Bay" is one of the minor masterpieces of our language—but who are these people, who are their neighbors, what is the world they belong to? We can scarcely guess. Too self sufficiently they drop out of the sky and fill the little canvas. There is no silent character in the background. True there is the mystery of life and death, suggested by the grandmother's memories of her dead son. But in a story like Chekhov's "The Steppe" there is something else besides the mystery of life and death: Russia, the condition of Russia, is the silent character always haunting us.

Commenting on Pritchett's criticism, Alpers (pp. 322ff.) writes:

> A perceptive critic puts a finger on the very spot and misses the point. *Of course* there are no "others" in Katherine Mansfield's New Zealand Stories. The "silent character" she was called on to present, whether in "At the Bay" or in its predecessor "Prelude," was not a human society but the lack of one. The silent character was the stillness of the bush, the disdain of the lofty islands for their huddled little pockets of colonial intruders, the silence of the vast sea-desert that encircle them.
>
> In 1893, when the real "Burnell family" moved from Thorndon to Karori, they were not moving, as a similar family might have moved in England, into a ready-made environment containing "neighbors." They were moving into a valley which only fifty years earlier had been covered with a dense forest, and which now was sparsely populated with colonists, uprooted, like themselves, from well defined English social strata, who had not yet learned how to live together. A measure of the Beauchamps' awareness of what they were doing is the fact that they took, in effect, another family with them to keep them company. When later they crossed the harbour to the summer colony at Day's Bay, to hold the festival of Christmas in the broiling sun, once again, "too self-sufficiently," they and their neighbours had to fill the little canvas for themselves. It was this, their loneliness and spiritual deprivation, that enabled Katherine Mansfield to pity her people at last; and this that she had to use as the "indispensable element" of her story.
>
> It was her duty, her object, and her achievement to do the same for her "undiscovered country" as Chekhov helped to do for Mother Russia. That having done so she should prompt a noted English critic to inquire "What is this world?" is only to prove that she had introduced a new human experience to literature: an experience which, however perplexing it may be to the Old World mind, remains entirely valid as material for literature.

Katherine Mansfield's strong personal sense of isolation and exile is pointed out by all of her biographers and critics. As an adolescent in New Zealand, she felt exiled from the culture of the Continent; in later life she felt exiled from her own homeland to which she longed to return. As an artist she felt exiled from mankind, and by her illness she felt exiled from the activities of normal life. Before entering the Gurdieff Institute (October 16, 1922), where she hoped to become well, she wrote in her *Journal* (p. 334) on October 14, 1922,

> But warm, eager, living life—to be rooted in life—to learn, to desire to know, to feel, to think, to act. This is what I want. And nothing less will do. That is what I must try for.

2. Katherine Mansfield, "Prelude" in *Selected Stories* edited and with an introduction by Elizabeth Bowen, New York, 1956, p. 65. Future references to this edition of stories are made in the text.
3. One of the most characteristic things about Katherine Mansfield's writing is the rapidity with which shifts in time, shifts in point of view from one character to another and shifts in the feelings of one person are made. V. S. Pritchett in *New Statesman and Nation*, XXXI, 87, comments on

> the grace with which she drops dramatically back into the past or slides into the thoughts and daydreams of her characters. Her writing changes its landscapes as noiselessly as they are changed in our minds and with the alacrity of Nature. . . . All these subtle changes which another writer would analyze, argue, or edge with a moral, glance and flutter with the freedom of a bird passing through sunlight and shadow.

Ian A. Gordon in *Katherine Mansfield*, London, 1954, pp. 21ff., discusses the ease and speed with which transitions are made.
4. The same characters reappear in Katherine Mansfield's short stories. "Prelude," "At the Bay," and "The Doll's House" were at one time to have been parts of novels (*Journal*, p. 262), and therefore would include the same characters. These are the three stories about the Burnells. But in all of the New Zealand stories the characters—the Burnells, the Sheridans, the Hammonds—are very much the same although the names vary. This is because Katherine Mansfield based the characters in these stories on her own family. Alpers traces the relationship between the names of the fictional characters and the names of members of Miss Mansfield's family (pp. 217ff.). Ian A. Gordon (p. 26) also relates the characters to members of the author's family and points out that the characters, particularly the husband and wife, age from "Prelude" through "Six Years After":

> This illumination of one story by another is particularly evident in the New Zealand family sequence, which, when read *as* a sequence, not in the order of composition but in the internal time-order of the family's own history, is one of the most sensitive and finely-conceived writings of our time.

5. I have paraphrased an expression taken from a letter, dated October 1920, which Katherine Mansfield wrote to John Middleton Murry: "I believe the greatest failing of all is to be frightened. Perfect Love casteth out Fear." (*Letters*, p. 334.) In a letter written to Richard Murry (brother of John Middleton Murry), dated February 1920, Katherine Mansfield stated her belief in the necessity of love in this way:

> Why should one love? No reason; it's just a mystery. But it is like light. I can only truly see in its rays. That is vague enough, isn't it? I do think one must (we must) have some big thing to live by, and one reason for the great poverty of Art today is that artists have got no religion and they are, in the words of the Bible, sheep without a shepherd. . . . We are priests after all. I fail and waver and faint by the way, but my faith is this queer *Love*. (*Letters*, p. 299.)

In another letter to Richard Murry, dated August 9, 1921, she again expresses her belief that only love casts out fear and therefore makes a person free (*Letters*, p. 394).

Chapter II

ℰℭ

The Private Inner World

Escape From Death

The objective world, then, does not provide a common ground for communication between Katherine Mansfield's characters. Also the characters have many different and often distorted views of each other and, in as much as all of the other characters are part of the objective world for any one character, all views of the objective world are necessarily entirely subjective. The objective world is negligible on three counts. In the first place human relationships have little reference to the objective world. As has been pointed out in the preceding chapter, each character responds to his own swiftly changing emotions and only ostensibly responds to other characters. In the second place there is no objective, cause-and-effect "real" world presented by the author. The stories are a series of subjective views of reality. By use of the interior monologue technique, the objective world is regularly seen through the conscious mind of the character and is subject to the distortions or prism of that particular sensibility.[1] In the third place, the characters themselves outrightly reject the objective world and the implications of human relationships for internal worlds where states of feeling predominate and govern.

Linda Burnell rejects her children and her husband and is inwardly occupied with a dream of pleasant escape. In "Prelude," she dreams of escaping in a carriage, but the usual symbol of her escape is a ship (p. 66). In "At the Bay," she dreams of taking an adventurous trip on a river boat in China with her father (p. 115). In the evening, standing before the aloe with her mother, Linda sees the aloe as a ship which will carry her away from Stanley and the children:

> She dreamed that she was caught up out of the cold water into the ship with the lifted oars and the budding mast. Now the oars fell striking quickly, quickly. They rowed far away over the top of the garden trees, the paddocks and the dark bush beyond. Ah, she heard herself cry: "Faster! Faster!" to those who were rowing. ("Prelude," p. 92.)

This erotic dream, which combines both masculine and feminine Freudian symbols, is more real to Linda than the actuality of her husband and children. Human life is terrifying to Linda and she fights against it. In "Prelude," she has a dream in which she is a young girl; her father gives her a little bird to hold, but the bird changes: its head swells and it becomes a human baby which she promptly drops into her apron (p. 65). Linda dreams of escaping not only her present life but all of life. She tries to transcend the mutability of life, time and death. What she fights against is the Bergsonian concept of life in which ebb and flow and change are reality.[2] She is unable to accept either the creative or destructive aspects of life which directly involve her. She dreams of a kind of Nirvana which will be free from all sensations and impressions and give an absolute, infinite peace. And like an enigmatic Buddha, she smiles when absorbed in this dream. Alone in the garden, she thinks:

> If only one had time to look at these flowers long enough, time to get over the sense of novelty and strangeness, time to know them! But as soon as one paused to part the petals, to discover the underside of the leaf, along came Life and one was swept away. And lying in her cane chair, Linda felt so light; she felt like a leaf. Along came Life like a wind and she was seized and shaken; she had to go. Oh dear, would it always be so? Was there no escape? ("At the Bay," p. 115.)

The gesture of parting the petals and finding life is similar to her father's parting the grasses (in the dream) and finding the little bird which is destroyed when it changes into human life. In both dreams Linda imagines herself outside of life—rowing over the trees and like a leaf in the air—suspended in a state of pure passivity.

Like Linda, Beryl withdraws from the objective world into a subjective, private one which is more real and more meaningful to her. While Linda dreams of the past, Beryl dreams of the future. If she had money of her own she would literally escape from the Burnell family ("Prelude," p. 63). While Linda feels pushed and pulled by "life" and dreams of escape to a perfect quiet, Beryl has the opposite set of feelings and dreams of a life of excitement. She feels trapped in her present situation; she fears being caught in the dull life away from the social life of the town ("At the Bay," pp. 71-72). She doesn't want to be "left" an old maid ("At the Bay," pp. 134-135). Unlike Linda who dreams of stillness, Beryl dreams of vivid impressions, novelty, and the strangeness of the unknown from which Linda retreats. In the present situation, Beryl feels she is acting a part and not being her "real" self. She feels that a lover is the only possible means of escape from her present life and the means by which she can realize her "real" self:

> She saw the real Beryl—a shadow . . . a shadow. Faint and unsubstantial she shone. What was there of her except the radiance? And for what tiny moments she was really she. Beryl could almost remember every one of them. At these times she had felt: "Life is rich and mysterious and good, and I am rich and mysterious and good, too." Shall I ever be that Beryl for ever? Shall I? How can I? And was there ever a time when I did not have a false self? ("Prelude," p. 98.)

Alone, particularly in the evening, Beryl feels as though the spirit of her unknown lover presides over the scene and watches her and they carry on imaginary conversations ("Prelude," pp. 78-80, and "At the Bay," p. 134). The unknown tempts Beryl and yearning for excitement she tries flirting with Stanley ("Prelude," p. 98). In "At the Bay," she momentarily considers Harry Kember's invitation to go into the garden with him (p. 136). Linda and Beryl, like most of the other characters see a split or duality between their inner and outer selves. The inner world is pleasant and the outer world is unpleasant and therefore unreal to them. They make distinctions between what they think is real and what is unreal in their worlds and seek the former. In "At the Bay," Jonathan Trout sees a sharp split in his world and wants to escape from his humdrum office job and explore the "vast dangerous garden of life" (p. 130). John

Hammond in "The Stranger," takes no cues from the objective world and until the end of the story lives in a pleasant dream of hoped for fulfillment. Each one refuses to accept change and death. Even Beryl is afraid she'll be caught and be an old maid. She feels "buried" in the new house ("Prelude," p. 95) and creates a private world to his own liking.

Escape From Loss of Love

Not only the adults but the children as well see a sharp distinction between their own world and the objective world (which, for the children, is the world of adults). Because they are children, their own world is different, of course, but Katherine Mansfield's children find the adult world hostile to them except for that portion of it associated with Grandmother Fairfield. It is the lack of communication between parent and child, discussed in Chapter I, which makes the adult world inimical to the child. Because the children feel rejected by their mother, they make a distinct effort to get away from the loveless adult world. Unlike the adults who reject the objective world willingly, the children are forced out of it. The adult world is so horrible that they enjoy getting away by themselves. Aunt Beryl who forever scolds and criticizes them in "Prelude," "At the Bay," and "The Doll's House," is a villain in their eyes. Mrs. Samuel Josephs' lady-help, who blows a loud whistle, organizes competitive games for the children, and gives parties where the Burnells usually end up getting water poured down their backs is particularly distasteful ("At the Bay," pp. 108-109). These two adults actively intrude into the children's world. In "At the Bay," the children go out to the wash-house to play games so as not to be disturbed by the adults. The children are torn between their desire for love and security from the adults and the drive to escape from the lack of it. Seeking love, they find it neither with nor away from adults. In "Sun and Moon," Sun's final gesture is typical. After not being able to understand why his father is suddenly so cross with him, he goes stomping back to the nursery, his own child's world (p. 195).

Katherine Mansfield's children try to escape a reality which includes a fear of the loss of love, and also the fear of death, change, and spoilage. The children and adults share the same fear of death. Sun cannot bear the sight of the ice house melted and the party decorations spoiled. Kezia, in "Prelude," is horrified by the decapitated duck. While the other children think the headless duck an amusing spectacle, Kezia is terrified and pleads with Pat to restore the duck's head. But when Pat picks her up in her arms, she is distracted by Pat's earrings and forgets about death (pp. 86-87). A similar distraction from death occurs in "At the Bay," when Kezia demands a promise from her grandmother that the grandmother will never die. Her death would mean that Kezia would be left without a source of love. They have been talking about Uncle William, who died long ago in Australia, and Kezia is prompted by her grandmother's reminiscing to ask if everybody has to die and why everybody has to die. The grandmother evades the question and distracts the child's attention by playing with her (pp. 119-120). Again distraction provides an escape from the reality of death for the child.[3]

At this point something about the character of the grandmother should be said because she has a stronger grip on the objective world than any of the other characters. And this is precisely because she accepts death and does not try to reject or escape from death into a private world. She knows that Uncle William died because "life is like that" ("At the Bay," p. 119). In "The Voyage," the grandmother, the seasoned traveller who takes the upper berth and who knows that "Our dear Lord is with us when we are at sea even more than when we are on dry land," accepts the inevitability of death and is not overwhelmed by it (pp. 280-281). Because the character of the grandmother in both stories does not try to transcend the human condition, she is at home in the natural world. In "Prelude," as soon as the grandmother steps into the new kitchen where she immediately sets things in order in a series of patterns, the natural world appears:

> She had noticed yesterday that a few tiny corkscrew tendrils had come right through some cracks in the scullery ceiling and all the windows of the lean-to had a think frill of ruffled green (p. 69).

The grandmother's reality which is solidly grounded in the natural world is contrasted with Linda's slight grip in the objective world in the scene where they both look at the aloe. Linda interrupts her own preoccupation with escape to ask her mother what she has been thinking and the old woman answers:

> I haven't really been thinking of anything. I wondered as we passed the orchard what the fruit trees were like and whether we should be able to make jam this autumn. There are splendid healthy currant

bushes in the vegetable garden. I noticed them today. I should like to
see those pantry shelves thoroughly well stacked with our own jam. . . .
("Prelude," p. 94.)

The grandmother's homey reality is typified by the gesture of "casting
on." She carries knitting with her and whenever her attention is not
required, her hand reaches for the ball of yarn ("At the Bay," pp. 110,
119). In contrast, Linda who cannot accept, is always "casting off."

In "Prelude," just before she drives away from the old house where
Lottie and Kezia are being left, she happily imagines she is "casting off"
the children (p. 53). She is like the mother in "Sun and Moon" who only
had time to say: "Out of my way, children!" (p. 189). It is only the
grandmother who, among the adults, does not reject the children, and
who does not desire to escape from her present life.

Subjective Worlds

Reality is entirely relative and depends upon the subject rather than
the object. As has been pointed out the lack of communication between
characters prevents the characters from sharing a common objective world.
In addition, the characters reject the objective world and escape into a
subjective one. These subjective worlds have little in common. To
further complicate the problem, the subjective world itself is unstable
and continually shifting and changing. Each character whose conscious
mind is seen is an intermediary between the reader and the subjective
world which the character inhabits. The stories are a series of subjective
views of reality. Objects are seen through the eyes of the character and
have a negligible objective existence. The values of objects change
according to the state of mind or feelings of the character concerned.
The object corresponds to or symbolizes a state of feeling, as the aloe
symbolizes Linda's dream of escape in a ship ("Prelude," p. 92). But
for Kezia, who looks at the aloe earlier in the day, it is strangely ugly
and because this grotesque plant corresponds to her mother's curt answers
about it, it symbolizes parental rejection (p. 75). The two mother-daughter
sets, Kezia-Linda and Linda-Mrs. Fairfield, have completely different
reactions to the aloe. Depending on personal feelings, the aloe is different
to each. To Linda, Mrs. Fairfield says: "I believe it is going to flower
this year. Look at the top there. Are those buds, or is it only an effect

of light?" ("Prelude," p. 92.) Mrs. Fairfield sees the flowering, life-bearing, beautiful aspect of the plant, but Linda sees the aloe as an invincible defense against her husband:

> Looking at it from below she could see the long sharp thorns that edged the aloe leaves, and at the sight of them her heart grew hard. . . . She particularly liked the long sharp thorns. . . . Nobody would dare to come near the ship or follow after. ("Prelude," p. 93.)

Stanley's neglect of the aloe is significant. On his way home from work, he is in such a hurry that the carriage speeds through the open gates, up the drive, and past the island where the aloe grows ("Prelude," p. 77). Stanley dashes past the aloe but never, in his characteristically unperceptive way, sees it. The aloe is a kind of reality principle which contains the dual aspects of nature. It has cruel thorny leaves but a fleshy stem which bears a blossom every hundred years. The duality it represents is only suggested, but were it stated it would be something like the duality between Beauty and Death. No one character grasps all the aspects of the plant; to each one it symbolizes something different.

Not only does the same object represent different things to different people, but an object changes value for one person depending on that person's feelings. Laura, going out to give directions to the men putting up the marquee, carries a piece of bread and butter in her hand ("The Garden Party," p. 286). Knowing that her mother would not ordinarily approve, Laura feels she has an excuse for eating out of doors; but as soon as she confronts the workmen and tries to give authoritative directions, she feels awkward. The bread and butter corresponds to this feeling and she tries to hide it. Then she realizes how friendly the workmen are. She begins to apologize for her superior social standing, and the bread and butter in her hand makes her feel at home with the workmen—like a work girl (p. 258).

Objects referred to in the stories have the function of provoking a state of feeling. They are imbued with a special quality given them by the observer. They come alive and take on new meaning for the character.[4] Nature is humanized and hovers in the background with a kind of quivering exciting life which manifests itself to a character when the character is alone. To Kezia, the stars in the night sky appear as cats' eyes ("Prelude," p. 62). In "The Garden Party," the roses have the capacity to understand that roses are the only flowers that impress people at garden parties (p.

285). In "Prelude," as Kezia approaches the new house in the storeman's wagon, she sees the inside of the house suddenly light up as someone carries a lamp through the empty rooms. The house quivers with life and sends out ripples of excitement (p. 59). Inside the house, the lamp which the grandmother gives to Kezia seems to breathe (p. 60). Linda, alone, listens to the silence spinning its web (p. 69).

Not only do physical objects take on a special significance when the character is alone, but the whole atmosphere comes alive.[5] These objects which respond as though alive, become very dear to the character concerned.[6] Each one of the Burnells desperately wants his own possessions to himself. In "At the Bay," Stanley wants a piece of the ocean to himself for his early morning swim (p. 102) he wants to keep his hat and walking stick to himself (p. 106). When he goes to work the women possess the "whole perfect day" for themselves (p. 107). It is understood that the women and children have the beach to themselves at eleven o'clock and at this time Linda has the lawn to herself (p. 110). The children (p. 124) go to the wash-house which they have for themselves. Alice has the afternoon to herself (p. 121) and Mrs. Stubbs, freed by her husband's death, has her life to herself (p. 124). Beryl is a most ardent possessor of her own room:

Why does one feel so different at night? Why is it so exciting to be awake when everybody else is asleep? Late—it is very late! And yet every moment you feel more and more wakeful, as though you were slowly, almost with every breath, waking up into a new, wonderful, far more thrilling and exciting world than the daylight one. And what is this queer sensation that you're a conspirator? Lightly, stealthily you move about your room. You take something off the dressing table and put it down again with a sound. And everything, even the bedpost, knows you, responds, shares your secret. . . .

You're not very fond of your room by day. You never think about it. You're in and out, the door opens and slams, the cupboard creaks. You sit down on the side of your bed, change your shoes and dash out again. A dive down to the glass, two pins in your hair, powder your nose and off again. But now it's suddenly dear to you. It's a darling little funny room. It's yours. Oh, what a joy it is to own things! Mine—my own! ("At the Bay," p. 133).

Beryl possesses her own room and the bedpost responds in a way which gives identity to Beryl's private or what she calls her "real" self. Since the characters do not find meaning in human relationships and try to escape them, they likewise forsake the identity which these relationships give them and are put upon to find another identity for the self in the subjective world. If Linda rejects the idea of herself as a mother, she must define herself in some other way and this other way is through the objects which she "possesses," the objects which respond to her, and which define her sense of herself. All of the characters find their separate identities through objects which they themselves imbue with special meaning. The objects take the place of human relationships and are far more responsive than people, just as Beryl's bedpost is more responsive to her (in her eyes) than the members of her family. But the bedpost can only be thought to respond with Beryl's own misplaced emotion. The emotion she, like the other characters, withdraws from human contact, she expends when alone on inanimate objects. For this reason, the private world is the whole universe to each character. Each character views the world as himself "writ large," so to speak. Emotional fragments are let loose and are lodged in inanimate objects or in nature. The characters do not have a human locus for their affections so that emotional investments are made, not in people, but in things which become unusually significant to the character. The character, thus, furnishes the world with himself and is really responding to his own free floating emotions rather than something in the objective world.[7] Even Laura, who does not reject the objective world to the extent that Beryl does, has an experience similar to Beryl's in the bedroom. After a telephone call, Laura sits and muses:

But the air! If you stopped to notice, was the air always like this? Little faint winds were playing chase, in at the tops of the windows, out at the doors. And there were two tiny spots of sun, one on the inkpot, one on a silver photograph frame, playing too. Darling little spots. Especially the one on the inkpot lid. It was quite warm. A warm little silver star. She could have kissed it. ("The Garden Party," p. 289.)

Notes

1. Berkman has an excellent discussion of Katherine Mansfield's first use of the interior monologue technique in "The Tiredness of Rosabel" written in 1908 (pp. 45-47), of her subsequent development and use of this technique (pp. 80-82), and of the way this technique was used by James Joyce, Virginia Woolf, and Katherine Mansfield (pp. 178-179).
2. According to John Middleton Murry in his autobiography, *Between Two Worlds*, London, 1935, p. 185, he was called "a brilliant young Bergsonian" by W. L. George and others of the group which centered around Dan Ryder's Bookshop in St. Martin's Lane, London, at the time he met Katherine Mansfield in 1911. Although there is no reference to indicate that she read Bergson, she must have known something of his ideas. In her *Journal* for February 1920, (pp. 202-203) Katherine Mansfield has the following entry which conveys an experience very much like the one Linda desires to have:

   And yet one has these "glimpses," before which all that one ever has written (what has one written?)—all (yes, all) that one ever has read, pales. . . . The waves, as I rode home this afternoon, and the high foam, how it was suspended in the air before it fell. . . . What is it that happens in that moment of suspension? It is timeless. In that moment (What *do* I mean?) the whole of life of the soul is contained. One is flung up—out of life—one is "held," and then,—down, bright, broken, glittering on to the rocks, tosses back, part of the ebb and flow.

3. In "The Garden Party," Laura is also distracted from death by her mother but the difference here is that Laura wants to face death whereas Kezia wants assurance that death can be escaped.
4. Louise Bogan in her essay, "Childhood's False Eden" in *Selected Criticism*, New York, 1955, pp. 186-187, quotes from an unidentified French translator, with regard to Katherine Mansfield, that

   She had the privilege of living in a Fairyland in the midst of a strange little phantasmagoria of which she was at once the creator and the dupe; in a little universe of her own where familiar objects . . . took on unexpected roles.

Miss Bogan's criticism of Katherine Mansfield's work is that it is unreal because it is an attempt (and it is implied that this attempt inevitably fails) to recreate childhood as Eden.

5. Katherine Mansfield herself felt that the atmosphere, or "silence" as she called it, hovered with life just hidden from apprehension. In a letter to John Middleton Murry, dated October 1920 (*Letters*, p. 333), she expresses this feeling, After saying that de la Mare shares her joy in the "silent world," she goes on to say:

> You know, I have felt very often lately as though the silence had some meaning beyond these signs, these intimations. Isn't it possible that if one yielded there is a whole world into which one is received? It is so near and yet I am conscious that I hold back from giving myself to it. What is this something mysterious that waits—that beckons?

Elizabeth Drew in *The Modern Novel*, New York, 1926, p. 247, comments on the unusual reality of Katherine Mansfield's stories:

> Where existence becomes a drop of water seen under the microscope, a substance teaming with unsuspected activity, where the reader lives in a tensity of feeling, a keenness of perception and a pitch of sensitiveness—a completely heightened reality—which makes normal life seem nothing but a shapeless blur.

6. Willa Cather, in *Not Under Forty*, New York, 1936, pp. 135-136, states that the desire of each character to possess something of his own is due to the fact that each character wants to be assured he is a self.

> Yet every individual in that household (even the children) is clinging passionately to his individual soul, is in terror of losing it in the general family flavor. As in most families, the mere struggle to have anything of one's own, to be one's self at all, creates an element of strain which keeps everyone almost at breaking point.

7. Daiches (pp. 70-73) discusses reality in Katherine Mansfield's work and the reasons why in her stories reality is so unlike what might be considered conventional reality in which objects have fixed values. He discusses her work in its temporal context.

> Truth viewed in terms of conventions and assumptions of a stable civilization ceased to be regarded as truth when it became obvious that that civilization was losing its stability, when its criteria of value were ceasing to be universal, and when its

conventions were coming to be viewed as irrelevant. Consciousness of the arbitrary nature of any such "classical" standard of truth in fiction, together with growing interest in psychology and the increase in self-awareness that psychological knowledge was bringing, resulted in the complete realization on the part of more sensitive writers of the false objectivity involved in the traditional approach to technique. The consequent attempt to discount these distorting factors in selection, observation, and method of recording led to a controlled, but nonetheless personal, delicacy of response to detail. This, as in Katherine Mansfield's case, had implications for technique as well as attitude. There came a shift in emphasis in the whole organization of narrative. Objective truth having been discredited—shown up as anything but objective—that author who was aware of, and sensitive to, contemporary currents of thought was led either to be a scientist, as he fondly thought, using psychology as his science, or else to depend on a personal sense of truth as Katherine Mansfield did.

* * * * *

Yet the aim is always to get completely outside one's self. The mind must be perfectly clear glass through which objective truth can pass undistorted. Then the personal sense of truth will correspond with reality. This doctrine involves the cultivation of a certain type of sensitivity to a point where observation or recollection is sufficient to set in motion a whole set of value judgments with their implications. The observer is confident that his reactions represent some kind of ultimate correspondence with what is observed or recollected.

What is this sensitivity that Katherine Mansfield cultivated so deliberately, to the point where it tended to defeat itself? It is simply an ability to see in objects what others, not possessed of this sensitivity, are unable to see; an ability to see as symbols objects which to others are not symbols at all or are symbols of more obvious things. It implies a quality in the observer and does not refer to anything in the thing observed. The potentiality for arousing emotion possessed by an object depends entirely on the mind of the observer of the object, not at all on inherent qualities in the object.

Reference is made to Katherine Mansfield's own statement on this point: "That which suggests the subject to the artist is the *unlikeness* to what we accept as reality. We single out—we bring into the light—we put up higher." For full quote see, Notes to Chapter I, n. 1.

Chapter III

ಬಿಂಡ

A Dual Reality: Conflict Between Dark and Light

Conflict Within the Subjective World

Not only does each character have a conflict between the objective world and his own subjective world, but also each has a conflict within the subjective world. The private world is built up as a defense against the mutability of the objective world, but its defenses cannot stand—it is fraught with danger both externally and internally. The dream world of escape has an obverse, dark side which is perhaps more terrifying than the aspects of the objective world from which the character desires escape. Because of this, the dual aspects of the subjective world clash in a sharpness which is far more vivid and horrible to the character than any discordant elements in the objective world. Linda is possessed by a nightmarish vision of things coming alive to frighten her:

> But the strangest part of this coming alive of things was what they did. They listened, they seemed to swell out with some mysterious important content, and when they were full she felt that they smiled. But it was not for her, only, their sly secret smile; they were members of a secret

society and they smiled among themselves. Sometimes, when she had fallen asleep in the daytime, she woke and could not lift a finger, could not even turn her eyes to left or right because THEY were there; sometimes when she went out of a room and left it empty, she knew as she clicked the door to that THEY were filling it. And there were times in the evenings when she was upstairs, perhaps, and everybody else was down, when she could hardly escape from them. Then she could not hurry, she could not hum a tune; if she tried to say ever so carelessly—"Bother that old thimble"—THEY were not deceived. THEY knew how frightened she was; THEY saw how she turned her head away as she passed the mirror. What Linda always felt was that THEY wanted something of her, and she knew that if she gave herself up and was quiet, more than quiet, silent, motionless, something would really happen. ("Prelude," p. 68.)

This is the unpleasant side of Linda's subjective world. The curious thing about "THEY" is the smile and the fact that the smile expresses something hidden, something which Linda finds withheld and ungraspable. "THEY" do the same thing to her which she does to her children—that is, she withholds from them and smiles. She makes the world mysterious and frightening to them by withholding love. Kezia knows what her mother's smile means and she knows that it is only the grandmother's love which dispells her fear of darkness. "THEY" leave Linda "out in the cold" just as she leaves Stanley out in the cold and forces him to ask repeatedly his characteristic questions: "Nothing wrong is there?" and "What are you smiling at?". The "THEY" are very much like Linda herself and do to her what she does to her husband and children. The smile functions as an image of withdrawal, rejection, and failure to communicate.[1] It is not only reality or the objective world which intrudes on Linda's pleasant escape world; it is also this hellish dream which possesses her and forces her into a kind of blindness which makes her unable to see or look in the mirror. She is as equally blind to the swelling impact of "THEY" as she is to her children.

John Hammond, in "The Stranger," who has built up a dream of reunion with his wife after her ten months' absence, has his dream destroyed less by reality than by another dream—a horrible one. An unbearable vision possesses John as he sits in an armchair which he imagines is draining his strength and imprisoning him. The overcoat across the bed looks to him like a headless corpse praying and the bed is described as blind (pp. 238-239). John has been blind to the fact that his wife has had some experience which has changed her in his absence. He mistakenly thinks that she hasn't changed at all and is exactly like she was when he had last seen her. He is blind to the inevitability of change in her as well as to death itself. Like Linda, who cannot look in the mirror when "THEY" surround her, and is temporarily blind, John is also blind. Death too, or the vision John has of death as a headless corpse, is blind or unknown just as "THEY" are blind to Linda's efforts to understand what "THEY" are smiling at. John tries to reject death, the stranger, the unknown, but what he rejects comes back in full force in the form of a dream and creates a private hell for him. Both John and Linda have an internal struggle with some dark, enigmatic spectre from which they cannot escape. The defenses of the pleasant dream world are constantly broken down, and the characters are shaped by what they reject or try to reject.

In "At the Bay," Beryl's struggle against the inimical forces of change is centered around her struggle with Harry Kember in the garden. Confrontation with Harry Kember destroys the vision of the lovely garden for Beryl. She had not counted on this serpent-like creature being in the garden which looked so lovely from her room. Harry Kember has a bright, blind, terrifying smile which paralyzes Beryl in horror. The shadows of the moon appear as prison bars of iron and it is difficult for her to believe she is in the same garden (pp. 135-137). Harry has very much the same effect on Beryl as "THEY" have on Linda or the vision of the headless corpse has on John Hammond or Linda has on Kezia: The image of the private smile and blindness function together to convey a sense of death, the unknown, and fear.

Like Beryl's struggle with the unpleasantness in the garden, Laura's struggle against death and darkness is centered in the dead carter and therefore occurs in the objective world. Darkness in the "The Garden Party" coalesces into the world of the Scotts just as light coalesces into the world of the Sheridans. After the party, Laura takes the basket of leftovers to the Scott's cottage. The moment she shuts her garden gate it grows suddenly dark and the alley through which she has to find her way is in "deep shade." She cannot quite realize that she is going somewhere where there is death but she tries to prepare herself for it. The sensations of the party are still with her as she sees people who look like shadows of death. She is frightened and thinks it a mistake to have come. She feels conspicuous in her bright party clothes and thinks she should have worn a coat to protect her against this world of darkness and the eyes of the staring bystanders. The woman who opens the cottage door is barely discernible in the murky light, and when Laura steps in she finds she cannot communicate with this woman with the oily smile. Laura wants to be saved from the nightmare she is in but the woman traps her in the passage (pp. 298-299). Laura's feeling of being trapped in a dark tunnel is like the image Linda has of childbirth being a journey down a dark tunnel ("At the Bay," p. 116). Kezia when told of Uncle William's death imagines a stiff figure beside a black hole ("At the Bay," p. 119), and Beryl knows the little pit of darkness beneath the fuschia bush where Harry Kember wants to take her ("At the Bay," p. 136). Only Laura is able to face this black tunnel without being completely overwhelmed; only she is able to accept death and does not try to escape. It is precisely because Laura accepts death that she is able to escape it, unlike any other character except the character of the grandmother.

The Dual Garden

A recurrent symbol of all that is horrible in life—death, change, spoilage, ugliness, etc.—is the dark side of the garden. Like the aloe, the garden is dual and contains life and death. It is the dark side of the garden from which the characters, except Laura and the grandmother, want to escape.[2] In "Prelude," the first morning in the new house, Kezia goes out to explore the garden which is divided into halves by the drive. The side with roses, daisies, fairy bells and other beautiful flowers is delightful to Kezia but the other side is frightening:

> On one side they all led to a tangle of tall dark trees and strange bushes with flat velvet leaves and feathery cream flowers that buzzed with flies when you shook them—this was the frightening side, and no garden at all. The little paths were wet and clayey with tree roots spanned across them like the marks of big fowl's feet. ("Prelude," p. 73.)

Kezia decides that this is no garden at all and is not tempted to explore it (p. 73). Mrs. Fairfield, looking at the vine which has poked its way into the kitchen, is reminded of the time when Beryl as a child had been stung by a red ant in the garden ("Prelude," p. 69). Although Mrs. Fairfield sees more life than death in the garden, she is aware that gardens are not altogether safe. When Linda sits in the garden with the new baby, she looks at the newly opened flowers and sees death. She wonders why they are made if they die as soon as they bloom ("At the Bay," p. 114). Time destroys everything and she laments the fact that there is not sufficient time to explore nature. Just as one parts the petals to examine the flower, one is whisked away by time and life. In "Prelude," she dreams of walking in a daisy field with her father, who bends down and parts the grasses to show her a baby bird. But what the garden has to offer is a baby bird which grows and swells into a human baby with an enormous head and knowing smile. This is so horrible to Linda (in her dream) that she drops the baby (p. 65). Like Beryl, Linda does not anticipate the dangers of change in the garden. Beryl actually explores the garden which Jonathan Trout only dreams of exploring in "At the Bay." Like Linda, he complains of not having sufficient time to explore nature which he calls a vast dangerous garden (p. 130). What the dangers are Beryl has the chance to discover. Like Jonathan she is tempted, but when the temptation is actually present, she runs away ("At the Bay," p. 137). Like Mrs. Kember's evil smile which both repels and attracts Beryl, the dark side of the garden is sometimes tempting. Stanley, who is unaware of the aloe is also unaware of the garden except for the fact that it is something for him to consume, part of the good bargain he got in the house. Like the beautiful weather, he thinks the garden was put at his disposal, that it is his as long as he pays for it ("Prelude," pp. 65-66).[3]

Linked with the symbol of the dual garden is the unknown. Those characters who fail to perceive or reject the dark side of the garden are utterly defeated. Knowledge of the dark side is inevitable and for those characters who persist in the illusion that this is not the case, this knowledge is fatal. This is true for all of the characters in " Prelude," "Sun and Moon," "The Stranger," and "At the Bay," except Mrs. Fairfield. What I have called the unknown is the inability to recognize the dark side of the garden as unknown and the unwillingness to explore or familiarize oneself with it. Kezia, who sees both aspects of the garden but who decides that the frightening side is no garden at all, is not afraid of getting lost because she decides that the dark side of the garden is no garden at all. The whole problem of not getting lost, finding one's way in the dark, knowing where one is, making the unknown familiar and recognizing change is not strictly related to the garden. It is symbolized by a journey through darkness but the meaning is closely associated with the symbol of the garden.

In "Prelude," the trip which Lottie and Kezia make in the storeman's dray to the new house is a trip through unknown territory. Every few minutes one of the children ask, "Where are we now?". It is at night and everything looks different; they feel lost. As they go over a hill, the things they pass disappear (pp. 57-58). When they finally arrive at the new house, the grandmother greets them with, "You found your way in the dark?" (p. 59). On the trip Lottie has fallen asleep but Kezia has kept wide awake looking and asking the storeman questions. The children sent out to play the first morning in the new house are described as minute puzzled explorers. In "At the Bay," when the children are frightened in the wash-house by the dark and by what they imagine to be a spider fallen from the ceiling, Kezia, although terrified, has to look with all her might (p. 127). She is like Laura who has to go everywhere and see everything ("The Garden Party," p. 294). Mrs. Fairfield has explored her new kitchen until every corner is familiar ("Prelude," p. 70).

Total Darkness and Total Light

There are some characters who do not live in a dual world, but who live in a world of total darkness. The Kembers, in "At the Bay," are two such people. They lead mysterious lives and the other people at the beach colony know little about them. Mrs. Kember has a narrow, exhausted looking face and withered hair, and although she lies in the sun all day it doesn't warm her (p. 111). She is lifeless and Beryl envisions Mrs. Kember dead after having been murdered by her husband (p. 112). Although Beryl is attracted to Mrs. Kember, she feels poisoned by her and filled with an evil feeling (pp. 113-114). Mr. Kember, too, is deathly—a sleep-walker (p. 112). In "The Garden Party," and "The Doll's House," the Scotts and the Kelveys occupy the black world of outsiders. Excluded by class discrimination, they are surrounded by death. Mrs. Scott's sister-in-law, with her swollen face, sly smile and oily voice, wears black and stands in the gloom ("The Garden Party," p. 299). Mrs. Scott, herself, is entombed in darkness out of which she cannot see:

> Her face, puffed up, red, with swollen eyes and swollen lips, looked terrible. She seemed as though she couldn't understand why Laura was there. What did it mean? Why was this stranger standing in the

kitchen with a basket? What was it all about? ("The Garden Party," p. 300).[4]

Like these people who see only one aspect of the dual world, there is another group who only see one aspect—the bright side. These people triumph in their rejection of death and live in an equally false or distorted world of total light. They have no conception of death and live in a kind of high noon light without shadow. Although the characters are unaware of it, they live in a parched, sunny world of drought. Stanley, Mrs. Stubbs, and Rags have no concept of death or at least a distorted concept. When Pat chops the duck's head off, Rags does not realize the duck is dead and he thinks he can keep just the head alive: "I don't think the head is quite dead yet," he said. "Do you think it would keep alive if I gave it something to drink?" ("Prelude," p. 87.) In "At the Bay," Mrs. Stubbs is more impressed by her husband's death than by his life. His love of large things is the one thing she remembers about him and she thinks that the fact he died of dropsy is a judgment on this love of largeness (p. 123). To her, his death does not so much mean that his life is over as that she is now free. Stanley Burnell also has very little concept of death and is associated with the sun. In "Prelude," he does his morning exercises in the exact center of a square of sunlight (p. 66). Thinking about his life in the new house, he decides that he would like to have a pew in church in the sun (p. 76). Linda is fond of Stanley in the daytime but hates him at night (p. 93).

To Mrs. Sheridan in "The Garden Party," death is unreal. When she hears about the accident her first concern is where it occurred; but as long as the accident has not occurred in her garden, it just doesn't exist. In answer to Laura's question as to whether the party should be postponed because of the death, she says:

> But my dear child, use your common sense. It's only by accident we've heard of it. If some one had died there normally—and I can't understand how they keep alive in those poky little holes—we should still be having our party, shouldn't we? ("The Garden Party," p. 295).

Mrs. Sheridan diverts Laura's attention from the death, and the issue does not come up again until Mrs. Sheridan thinks it would be a brilliant idea to send the widow some of the party leftovers (p. 297). She has so little concept of the life beyond her garden gate that she imagines the widow would be delighted to receive this gift. She thinks it will be helpful to the widow to have some food prepared for the people who will visit the cottage. Mrs. Sheridan wants to tell Laura not to look at the body, but somehow she can't quite bring herself to tell Laura not to look at something which she herself hardly believes exists (p. 298). Her values are so warped that death is successfully excluded. Her mind edits and censors all darkness.

The symbol of this world of false light is Laura's hat. By popping the hat on Laura's head, Mrs. Sheridan manages to divert Laura's attention from the death to how pretty she looks. She wants Laura to look at herself in the mirror, but at first Laura thinks her mother is all wrong and cannot do so. Finally, Laura does look in the mirror and is so taken by the view of herself in the hat that she begins to wonder whether her mother is right (p. 295). She decides to think about it after the party, but when she sees her brother, Laurie, she tries to ask him whether he thinks the party should be postponed. He is so taken by his sister in the hat that she cannot ask him. At the party, Laura is told repeatedly by the guests how becoming the hat is, how well she looks in it, that she looks Spanish, etc. (p. 296). After the party, her mother tells her to go dressed as she is to the dead man's cottage (p. 298). On the way down the dark alley, Laura wishes she had worn a hat which would have made her feel less conspicuous (p. 298). She feels that the hat gives her away and that the old woman with crutches and her feet on a newspaper is watching her and when she asks directions, she pushes the streamer off her shoulder. When Laura stands before death and looks at the smiling corpse, her only words are "forgive my hat" (p. 300). The hat symbolizes Mrs. Sheridan's world of false light. Wearing it, Laura does not feel worthy of seeing anything as beautiful as the "marvel" before her.

This world of false light is curiously sterile or deathly in its own way because it excludes death. In "At the Bay," it is associated with noon:

> The tide was out; the beach deserted; lazily flopped the warmed sea. The sun beat down, beat down hot and fiery on the fine sand, baking the grey and blue and black and white-veined pebbles. It sucked up the little drop of water that lay in the hollow of the curved shells; it bleached the pink convulvulus that threaded through and through the sand hills. Nothing seemed to move but the small sand-hoppers. (p. 117)

The little beach colony is baked in a hellish heat. Everyone is taking a midday nap and the road is empty except for the exhausted dog who seems to be waiting for a cart to come along and pick him up. The blinds of all the bungalows are closed and: "Over the verandahs, prone on the paddock, flung over the fences, there were exhausted-looking bathing dresses and rough striped towels." (p. 118.) Everything is deathly still and, inside the bungalow, Kezia and her grandmother have their discussion about death. It is significant that Uncle William died of sunstroke. The hot noon sun dries everything, burns, and makes all water evaporate. Either extreme of total darkness or total light is death.[5]

Notes

1. Wanda Darling, "Katherine Mansfield: Her Writing, Development, and Literary Effect," unpublished Master's thesis, Columbia University, 1941, pp. 25-27, here lists references to twenty-five different kinds of smiles. She criticizes the repetitive use of the word and does not comment on its function as an image or symbol. Celeste T. Wright in her article, "Katherine Mansfield and the Secret Smile," in *Literature and Psychology*, the Newsletter of the Conference on Literature and Psychology of the Modern Language Association (August 1955), pp. 44-48, refers to the smile used in the *Letter* and *Journal* as well as the *Stories*.
2. In a letter written to John Middleton Murry, dated October 29, 1919 (*Letters*, p. 230), Katherine Mansfield expresses a horror of this same kind of unpleasantness in the garden. "But . . . this vileness, this snail on the underside of the leaf—always there!"
3. Katherine Mansfield herself felt defeated by the horror of life. "But the ugliness—the ugliness of life—the intolerable corruption of it all—How is it to be borne?" she wrote to Lady Ottoline Morrell on May 24, 1918 (*Letters*, p. 157).
4. Celeste T. Wright, in "Darkness as a Symbol in Katherine Mansfield " *Modern Philology*, LI, 204-207 (February 1954) also discusses this matter.
5. The overpowering sense of death and the inability to cope with it which the characters in the New Zealand stories have is very much like Katherine Mansfield's own all-pervading sense of death. She wrote in her *Journal*, December 15, 1919 (p. 184), "All these two years I have been obsessed by the fear of death. This grew and grew and grew gigantic. . . ."

Chapter IV

୫୨୦ଛ

Reality: A Unity

The Reality of Darkness

I n "The Stranger," "Sun and Moon," and "At the Bay," destruction, from which the characters try to escape, is reality. Each character builds up his defenses against it and the more desperately he does so, the more triumphantly death overwhelms him. The fortifications against death and corruption are torn away; the character is left naked in the face of reality and able only to utter his cry against it. In "At the Bay," Stanley's early morning swim is ruined by Jonathan's presence (p. 103). Then Stanley's breakfast is spoiled because Beryl forgot the sugar for his tea (p. 104); not being able to find his hat and walking stick, he begins a day which is pure Hell (p. 132). He tortures himself all day for not saying goodbye to Linda, and when he discovers that she has been unaware of his intention to punish her or even of his neglect to say goodbye in the morning, he is hurt again. His homecoming, at which he had hoped to find forgiveness, is spoiled. Just as Stanley's swim in the morning has been spoiled, so was Jonathan's—he'd stayed in the water too long (p. 104). Not leaving the water sooner is the beginning of Jonathan's day, during which he is always late. He is late coming to pick up his two children (p. 128). He stays to talk with Linda who thinks he has come to borrow something because the Trouts are always running out of things and coming to borrow from the Burnells at the "last" moment. What Jonathan talks about is his sense of time running out and the fact that he has to spend the best years of his life sitting on a stool in the office from nine to five. Jonathan wants to escape time and destruction: "The shortness of life! The shortness of life! I've only one night or one day and there's this vast dangerous garden, waiting out there, undiscovered, unexplored." ("At the Bay," p. 130.) Linda asked Jonathan if it were not too late, even now, to escape, but he cried that he was too old. For the first time Linda saw Jonathan as weak and touched with age and she wonders:

> What was the matter with Jonathan? He had no ambition; she supposed that was it. And yet one felt he was gifted, exceptional. He was passionately fond of music; every spare penny he had went on books. He was always full of new ideas, schemes, plans. But nothing came of it all. The new fire blazed in Jonathan; you almost heard it roaring softly as he explained, described, and dilated on the new thing; but a moment later it had fallen in and there was nothing but ashes, and Jonathan went about with a look like hunger in his black eyes. ("At the Bay," p. 129.)

Jonathan, regretfully facing middle age, from which he cannot escape, wants desperately to "live," but instead, he is reminded by his graying hair that he must go on living the life of a prisoner or an insect banging its head against the wall in an attempt to escape. As Linda listens to Jonathan's cry against time and death, the sun sets and she thinks:

> Sometimes when those beams of light show in the sky they are very awful. They remind you that up there sits Jehovah, the jealous God, the Almighty, whose eye is upon you, ever watchful, never weary. You remember that at his coming the whole earth will shake into one ruined graveyard; the cold bright angels will drive you this way and that, and there will be no time to explain what could be explained so simply. . . . ("At the Bay," p. 131)

Death pervades this episode between Jonathan and Linda. The day dies, Jonathan stands on the darkening grass, his voice is shadowy and seems to Linda to boom from beneath the ground as though he were already dead like the new fire in him which "had turned" to ashes. He thinks of himself as a victim under circumstances to which he can never become accustomed.

The women, too, are faced with destruction. After Stanley had left for work in the morning, they think they have the whole perfect day to themselves. A symbolic murder is committed by Alice, the servant girl, who is washing the breakfast dishes:

> "Oh, these men!" said she, and she plunged the teapot into the bowl and held it under the water even after it had stopped bubbling, as if it too was a man and drowning was too good for them. (*"At the Bay,"* p. 107.)

But this is not the only time Alice encounters death on this day. At Mrs. Stubbs', where she has gone for tea on her free afternoon, Alice listens to Mrs. Stubbs talk about her husband's death. After Alice looks at photographs of the dead man and discovers that he died of dropsy and had to be drained of liquid, the very thought of which makes her jump, she wishes she were back in her own kitchen instead of listening to Mrs. Stubbs' deathly discussion (p. 124). Alice carries a sunshade which she calls her "PERISHALL" (p. 121).

Each successive encounter with death or destruction grows in intensity. This is not only because each encounter itself is with a more horrifying form of death, but also because each reference is intensified by the preceding references. The children look for "buried" treasure cast off from wrecks (p. 109). In the middle of the day Kezia and her grandmother discuss death, and later in the wash-house the children are terrified by the dark. Their game of animals has been spoiled. They see a face looking at them through a window and they shriek out in horror before they realize it is only Uncle Jonathan (p. 128).

Beryl is attracted by Mrs. Kember but at the same time this deathly woman fills Beryl with an evil feeling (p. 113). Beryl feels poisoned and imagines Mrs. Kember murdered by her husband (p. 112). Late at night when Beryl is in her room and dreaming about the lover who will take her away and save her from her present life, she sees Harry Kember approaching the house (p. 135). She has been looking out at the beautiful garden from her window. Even the stars seem to conspire with her in sharing the exciting night. When Harry Kember asks her to go for a walk with him she is very much tempted to do so and steps out into the garden. But as soon as she does so, the garden is completely changed and she thinks of the pit of darkness beneath the fuschia bush to which Harry Kember suggests they go (p. 136). This pit of darkness with a showering fuschia bush above is an image similar to several previous ones in the story. The pit is like the grave-like black hole beside which lies the stiff, dead body of Uncle William (p. 119). The shower is an image similar to Alice's holding the teapot/drowning man under the water (p. 107), as well as similar to the stream of water which Pip pours over the squashed boot he finds as buried treasure (p. 109). Lottie, sitting at the edge of the water, is frightened by a "whiskery" wave which threatens to shower her (p. 111). At the horrible parties which the Samuel Josephs give, the Burnell children usually end up getting something poured down their backs (p. 108). Any reference to a shower over anything is distasteful. Mr. Stubbs became a kind of tank which had to be drained before he died of dropsy (p. 123). Although the characters in "At the Bay" enjoy swimming, they all want to go in at their rate, and any premature showering is unpleasant and has a death-by-water connotation. When Beryl thinks of the pit of darkness under the bush in the garden which had looked so beautiful from the window of her room, the garden now looks very different to Beryl. "The moonlight stared and glittered; the shadows were like bars of iron" (p. 136). The garden prison image here is the same image Jonathan has of his life. Beryl is momentarily Harry Kember's victim.

Linda, like the other characters, is overwhelmed by death. Sitting in the garden and looking at the flowers on the manuka tree, she asks: "Who takes the trouble—or the joy—to make all these things that are wasted. . . . It was uncanny" ("At the Bay," p. 114). Time is the enemy which prevents her from examining the flowers and knowing nature.

Death, destruction, or corruption interferes in the life of each character and completely overwhelms him. Death is also the frightening power of the unknown. Each character in "At the Bay" not only builds up defenses against death but also struggles not to give himself away to the hidden darkness of the unknown. Although Jonathan dreams of discovering the vast, unexplored garden, he does not anticipate hidden dangers in the garden. Neither does Beryl until she is confronted by Harry Kember. Not anticipating danger in the unknown has terrible consequences, as Beryl discovers. Linda thinks of the "eye" of the Jehovah who is always watchful and knows something she does not know. She imagines the day of judgment as a time and situation in which she is unable to communicate, unable to explain or give an account of herself. The all-knowing eye is like the eye Alice imagines watching her as she leaves the house and walks to Mrs. Stubbs' (p. 121). Beryl is watching her, but Alice does not know this. She does not turn around and look but turns her back for fear of being discovered. She is afraid of giving herself up to her fear of the unknown. Beryl turns her back to Mrs. Kember's eyes as she undresses for swimming. She never undresses in front of anyone and feels that because Mrs. Kember is watching her that Mrs. Kember is discovering her and has some power over her. Beryl feels inexperienced in front of Mrs. Kember and feels that Mrs. Kember knows something about her which she doesn't know herself (pp. 111-113). Mrs. Kember is a sphinx-like character who knows about Beryl but is herself completely mysterious to Beryl. She advises Beryl to "enjoy life" and tells Beryl that it is a sin for her to wear clothes, since she has such a lovely figure. Beryl imagines that she would like to "enjoy life" and that it would be fascinating to have the kind of power over other people that Mrs. Kember has over her. Discovering that the unknown is not altogether pleasant, in spite of its tempting appearance, is what Beryl learns when she steps into the garden with Harry Kember. She had dreams of being discovered by a lover who would "save" her, but instead it is Harry Kember, out for a stroll, who discovers her.

Each character feels watched. The children playing in the wash-house are terrified by a watching face:

> Suddenly Lottie gave such a piercing scream that all of them jumped off the forms, all of them screamed too. "A face—a face looking!" shrieked Lottie.

> It was true, it was real. Pressed against the window was a pale face, black eyes, a black beard. ("At the Bay," pp. 127-128.)

Of course it turns out to be only Uncle Jonathan. But each character has the experience of being watched and discovered by a powerful eye. Each character fights against giving himself away and being discovered but is unsuccessful in the attempt. For each character the day is spoiled by death, the reality which each one tries to escape. In "The Stranger," John Hammond is completely overcome by death, and the thought that his wife has held a dying man in her arms makes him think that he and his wife will never be alone again. Death has come between them. The stranger here is both death and the unknown. The experience his wife has had is something which John will never share with her. "Sun and Moon" likewise ends with the destruction of Sun's vision of the ice house. The child's reality does not allow for change and he expects the party decorations to look the same after the party as they did before it.

Accepting Reality

"At the Bay" was written in September 1921 and although the former story was conceived as a continuation of "Prelude" (1917) and was supposed to be the second part of a projected novel, it is far more closely related to "The Garden Party." Anthologies of Katherine Mansfield's short stories follow a chronological order except for having "At the Bay" immediately following "Prelude." A consideration of "At the Bay" in relation to "The Garden Party" shows that something is lost in this arrangement. "The Garden Party" seems to me to be a resolution of the conflicts in "At the Bay," and therefore printing "At the Bay" immediately before "The Garden Party" would enhance this relationship. Both "Prelude" and "At the Bay" are about the same characters, the Burnells, but all of the New Zealand stories have the same or only slightly different characters reappearing in all the stories.[1] The relationship between "At the Bay" and "The Garden Party" is in the treatment of Death. Reality in "The Garden Party" is distinctly different from reality in "At the Bay."

Whereas in "At the Bay" (and in the stories preceding "At the Bay") death is rejected by each character; in "The Garden Party" it is accepted. Death in the former story is something to be feared and escaped but in the latter story it is not only accepted but beautiful. What the characters in "At the Bay" fail to come to terms with, Laura in "The Garden Party" succeeds in facing. Laura not only succeeds in accepting death, but she escapes the fear of death which haunts the characters in "At the Bay." Because she acknowledges the reality of death she is able to transcend the fear of it. This she does by transfiguring death into something beautiful—a marvel. The values of reality in the two stories are reversed, in "At the Bay" the very thought of death destroys life for each character who is made unhappy by it. Life is ruined by the thought of death, change, time and destruction. But in "The Garden Party" life is enhanced by death. Death not only enhances life but it makes life seem less beautiful than death. It is precisely the absence of death in Mrs. Sheridan's world which makes it so artificial. In "At the Bay" death is the enemy which destroys each character's dream, but in "The Garden Party" death is so beautiful that it makes life look lacking. As has been pointed out in Chapter III, Mrs. Sheridan's world is sterile and the emotional poverty there makes life less desirable than death. Here life destroys death, but in "At the Bay" death destroys life; darkness triumphs. In "At the Bay" each character looks upon death as an illusion and tries to build a dream world which excludes death. In "The Garden Party" death is a reality which is totally accepted and transmuted into beauty. Death spoils the natural world for the characters in "At the Bay" but in "The Garden Party" Laura finds beauty in the inevitability of death.[2]

Mrs. Sheridan's world of false light, which is the world of conventional reality, is false because it deletes death. It is a heartless world in which nature is withheld from all except Laura. The story opens with a description of the garden before the party. It is a perfect day in which nature aids and is at the disposal of the Sheridans. A halo of gold envelops the scene. The blue sky "was veiled with a haze of light gold" (p. 285). The opening is casual, conversational, and familiar but at the same time the scene is in some way special, as though the heavenly host were in the background. Even the bushes are bowed down in humility and reverence before the splendor of the natural world. The unique scene is where a garden party is about to take place. The contrast between the beauty offered by the natural world and the failure of the guests to see this beauty is immediately made. Significantly, we are told that the guests only "know" roses, and therefore no other flowers would "impress" them. The loveliness of the garden is withheld from the guests who come to be impressed rather than to see. Everything must be conspicuous or the guests will miss it. The workmen who come to put up the marquee are aware of the blatant pretentions of this world even more than Laura is. When Laura suggests that the marquee be put up on the lily lawn, one of them says, "You want to put it somewhere where it'll give you a bang slap in the eye, if you follow me" (p. 286). The workman suggests that a sufficiently conspicuous place would be against the karaka trees, but Laura thinks:

> Against the karakas, then the karaka trees would be hidden. And they were so lovely, with their broad, gleaming leaves, and their clusters of yellow fruit. They were like trees you imagined growing on a desert island, proud, solitary, lifting their leaves and fruits to the sun in a kind of silent splendour. Must they be hidden by a marquee? They must. ("The Garden Party," p. 287.)

When Laura sees the workman bend down and pinch a sprig of lavender to get to the smell of it, she thinks that the workman, caring for things like the smell of lavender, is very different different from her own friends who do not care for things like this (p. 287). For them the beauties of the natural world do not exist. Laura credits this situation to absurd class distinctions and conventions which she despises.

This world is not only unable to see the beauties of the natural world, but it perpetrates a sinister heartlessness which is repeatedly built up to the point where Mrs. Sheridan refuses to consider the death of the carter as real. During the preparations for the party, Laura's sister Jose, who loved to give orders to the servants as though she were acting a part in a drama, plays the piano unfeelingly: "And although the piano sounded more desperate than ever, her face broke into a brilliant, dreadfully unsympathetic smile." ("The Garden Party," p. 290.) Jose is less interested in the thing she is doing than in her own sense of superiority in doing it. Contrasted with Laura's shocked reaction at the news of the accident, Jose's reaction is completely cruel. When Laura pleads that they stop the party because of the accident, Jose says in amazement:

> Stop the garden party? My dear Laura, don't be absurd. Of course we can't do anything of the kind. Nobody expects us to. Don't be so extravagant. ("The Garden Party," p. 293.)

Mrs. Sheridan's reaction to the accident is similar to Jose's. She, too, persists in eliminating death from her world. Mrs. Sheridan succeeds in deleting death but at a price which makes her world deathly in its artificiality. Her world kills all feeling. That someone had the impertinence to die on the day of her party is a social error which polite society will do its best to overlook. Like Jose who lives as though she were acting a part in a play, Mrs. Sheridan lives a life in which her responses are nothing more than an acquired pose. What passes for feeling in her case is nothing more than the learned niceties of social behavior. When Mr. Sheridan mentions the accident after the party, Mrs. Sheridan thinks this is very tactless of her husband (p. 297). Death simply does not belong there.

But Laura, the heroine of the story, is different from the other members of the family. She is the "artistic" one who is sent out to give directions to the men putting up the marquee (p. 236). She is the only one who is affected by the accident, and when her mother suggests taking the left-overs to the party, the suggestion affects her differently than it does the rest of the family. Laura is set apart and unique in her capacity to feel:

Again, how curious, she seemed to be different from them all. To
take scraps from their party. Would the poor woman really like that?
("The Garden Party," p. 297.)

Laura questions her mother's attitude and wonders whether her mother
is right or wrong. But what makes Laura extraordinarily different from
her family and her family's friends is her capacity to accept everything.
She not only accepts the death of the carter and reacts to it, but she also
accepts her mother's distorted world. Laura is receptive to the beauties
of the natural world in a way which the other characters are not. Every
gesture Laura makes during the story is one of affirmation. Her sense of
the injustice of class distinctions does not prevent her from seeing that
the workman, who cares about the smell of the spring of lavender, has
the capacity to care which her family lacks. Because he cares, he is more
alive than her family and in the end has more of a sense of the earth than
they do. Class distinction does not deprive him of very much. The
Sheridan's by contrast have nothing—life eludes them because it is life
without death. In the midst of plenty they are starving and do not realize
it.

The first part of "The Garden Party," the scene of the Sheridan's
home and the party itself, contains the beauty of the natural world. The
image for the natural world on this afternoon is the flower. "And the
perfect afternoon slowly ripened, slowly faded, slowly its petals closed"
(p. 296). Within this beauty there is the Sheridan's world which, because
of its sterility, only gives the illusion of life. It is the blight within the
flower—it is a kind of death which prevents the characters from seeing
life or beauty. The false light in which they live is of their own creation,
their own determined efforts to delete death.

In the second part of "The Garden Party," the world of the alley and
the dead man, the natural world is completely dark, but natural death is
beautiful. Both scenes in the story have the parallels of death and beauty
but the parallels are reversed. In the first part the natural world is
beautiful in comparison to which life is deathly, but in the second part
the natural world is dark and ugly while actual death is magnificent.
Curiously, the people, except Laura, in both parts are more dead than
alive. They live either in the extreme of total light or total darkness both
of which extremes have the same consequences for the people. They are
all dead. Just as Mrs. Sheridan is unaware of the world beyond her
garden gate, the people in the alley are unaware of any world other than

their own. In fact, like Mrs. Sheridan who is unaware of the beauty of her own garden, these people in the alley are unaware not only of the Sheridan world, but also of the beauty of death before them. They have something which Mrs. Sheridan doesn't have, but like Mrs. Sheridan they too are unaware of what they *do* have.

Just as Laura accepts her mother's world, she also accepts the dark world of the Scotts and natural death. Once she closes her gate she steps into a dark world where she is the only light:

> Now the broad road was crossed. The lane began, smoky and dark. Women in shawls and men's tweed caps hurried by. Men hung over the palings; the children played in the doorways. A low hum came from the mean little cottages. In some of them there was a flicker of light, and a shadow, crab-like, moved across the window. Laura bent her head and hurried on. She wished now that she had put on a coat. How her frock shone! And the big hat with the velvet streamer—if only it was another hat! Were the people looking at her? They must be. It was a mistake to have come; she knew all along it was a mistake. Should she go back even now? ("The Garden Party," p. 298.)

Laura is frightened by the dark squalor, and having come from such brightness, she can hardly find her way in the dark. She feels she is losing her way and venturing farther than she would like to go. "Oh, to be away from this! She actually said, 'Help me, God'" (p. 299). But the point is that she does go on and does not run away. She makes her way as best she can and although the people smile queerly at her, she stops and asks directions. Laura's sense of being out of place and in the unknown is as terrifying to her as the squalor and darkness. She feels that all eyes along the road are on her, and although the figures of the people are indistinct to her, she knows that she is seen plainly. To be discovered by what she cannot understand is horrible. "To be away from those staring eyes, to be covered up in anything, one of those women' s shawls even" (p. 200). This situation is similar to one in which each character in "At the Bay" feels that an eye is upon him. The characters feel helpless before the all-seeking mysterious eye which catches them frightened. They feel naked and given away in their fright and left without an avenue of escape. But the difference between the characters in "At the Bay" and Laura is that Laura does not cry out in horror, she just keeps going: "I'll just leave the basket and go, she decided. I shan't even wait for it to be emptied" (p. 299). The characters in "At the Bay" do not escape a final sense of being trapped but Laura, who feels momentarily trapped in several instances, accepts the trap, and because she does she escapes it finally. Mrs. Sheridan traps Laura by the hat and diverts her attention from the death.[3] At first Laura cannot look at herself in the mirror but finally she does (p. 295). If Laura had her own way the party would be postponed but she gives way temporarily to her mother's wishes. Then when Laura arrives at the Scotts', she wants to leave the basket and not go in but she gets trapped in the passageway by Mrs. Scott's sister to whom Laura is unable to communicate. In the kitchen, "Laura only wanted to get out, to get away" (p. 300). The woman manages to get Laura into the bedroom where the dead man lies, and Laura passively follows her to the corpse. Laura doesn't want to look, but just as she finally looked in the mirror which her mother had held before her, she finally looks at death. Laura is the explorer who must see everything and go everywhere no matter how painful or sordid the place or thing may be.

Transcending Darkness

But what Laura finds in death is not desolation but fulfillment:

> There lay a young man, fast asleep—sleeping so soundly, so deeply, that he was far, far away from them both. Oh, so remote, so peaceful. He was dreaming. Never wake him up again. His head was sunk in the pillow, his eyes were closed; they were blind under the closed lids. He was given up to his dream. What did garden parties and baskets and lace frocks matter to him? He was far from all those things. He was wonderful, beautiful. While they were laughing and while the band was playing, this marvel had come to the lane. Happy . . . happy. . . . All is well, said the sleeping face. This is just as it should be. I am content. ("The Garden Party," p. 300.)

Laura painfully accepts death and transmutes it into something beautiful.[4] She does this not with resignation but with a sense of death being right— "just as it should be." It is precisely the necessary shadow of death in all things which is the beauty and mystery of life.

Because she accepts death, she does not fear its power over her. The eyes of death are closed, and unlike the staring eyes of the people in the street, these eyes do not discover her and make her desperately want to hide. In "At the Bay , " the characters feel helpless in the presence of an eye which discovers them and gives them away. The watching eyes in "At the Bay" have the terrifying power of the unknown over the characters. It is not the physical corpse which is beautiful to Laura as much as it is the wonderful mystery of the thing. Laura tells her brother, "It was simply marvellous" (p. 301). But the story does not end on death. Laura returns from her descent into darkness and comes through to her brother and Life. After seeing death, her exit from the dark world is made easily and without the difficulties of the journey to death. On the way back, having seen ultimate darkness, Laura knows her way and is not afraid of getting lost: "And this time she didn't wait for Em's sister. She found her way out the door, down the path, past all those dark people." ("The Garden Party," p. 300.) Out of the shadow steps her brother, the one member of her family with whom she can communicate (when he is not distracted by Laura' s hat—the symbol of their mother's artificial world) and with whom as a consequence she shares those explorations where "one must go everywhere; one must see everything" (p. 294), and not be overwhelmed by what one sees. Their conversation immediately turns to life—to which Laura has been reborn:

> "But Laurie—," she stopped, she looked at her brother. "Isn't life," she stammered, "isn't life." But what life was she couldn't explain. No matter. He quite understood. "Isn't it, darling?" said Laurie. ("The Garden Party," p. 301.)

Reality is light and life in both "The Garden Party" and "The Doll's House." But in both stories it is a reality in which light finally triumphs over darkness precisely because it depends on darkness being there and being accepted. In "The Doll's House," Else, the washerwoman's daughter whose only words in the whole story are the final ones: "I seen the little lamp," (p. 326) is similar to Laura in the way in which they both transcend darkness and apprehend beauty and light. The reality of both heroines includes darkness and light, and is a unity synthesized out of this diversity. Both heroines' vision penetrates through darkness or appearance and finally apprehends light, truth, or reality.[5]

"The Doll's House" is written in such a way that Else's words "I seen the little lamp" symbolizes some universality or truth similar to Laura's unstated vision of reality which compels her to ask: "isn't life?". What this lamp represents is not only indirectly suggested, but it is also difficult to apprehend and hidden to all but the pure in heart. After a series of unveilings are stripped away, the reader, like the Burnell children, finally sees the lamp. The doll's house, which is so heavy that two men must carry it, is kept in the courtyard and not taken into the house because Aunt Beryl objects to the smell of paint. "But the perfect, perfect little house! Who could possibly mind the smell? It was part of the joy, part of the newness." ("The Doll's House," p. 318.) The outside of the house is seen by the children, then the inside in all its detail; and finally Kezia sees the lamp—"an exquisite little amber lamp with a white globe" (p. 319). To Kezia the lamp was the best part of the house. The lamp was "real" and like lamps the children "burn" to tell their friends about the house (p. 319). It is Kezia who reminds her sister, Isabel, to tell their school friends about it (p. 322). Just as the doll's house is banished to the courtyard because of the smell, the Kelvey children are banished from the Burnell world because they are social outcasts—the children of a washerwoman and a gaolbird and not fit company for other people's children (p. 321). They smell, too. Like the lamp behind the housefront, Else Kelvey is seen behind her sister. Both the lamp and Else could easily be overlooked and are overlooked by Aunt Beryl. Else scarcely talks and accepts the abuse of the other children without defending herself. Else has "big, imploring eyes: (p. 324), and in her dumbness she is like the sorrowful bush which says to Beryl in "At the Bay," "We are dumb trees, reaching up in the night, imploring we know not what" (p. 134). And like the imploring bush, Else wants to see the doll's house when the opportunity arises (p. 324). She reaches up out of the dark outsider's world, and in spite of Beryl's success in dispelling them from the garden, Beryl cannot prevent Else's seeing the light. With every disadvantage Else overcomes darkness and sees the light.

The unfinished story, "Six Years After," is Katherine Mansfield's final expression of Reality. The wife continues to seek with the realization that she may never find. Knowing that there may be nothing more to life than final death, she goes on with the hope that there may be something else. Like Else and Laura, this woman has the capacity to see through darkness. But, as with Else and Laura, facing darkness is painful. At first she doesn't dare turn and look back at the lonely gulls, the sea, and the rain because after the steamer passes by there is nothing. She decides she won't look because it is too depressing:

> But immediately, she opened her eyes and looked again. Lonely birds, water lifting, white pale sky—how were they changed?

And it seemed to her there was a presence far out there, between the
sky and the water. Someone very desolate and longing watched them
pass and cried as if to stop them—but cried to her alone. ("Six Years
After," p. 346.)

The presence crying out is the memory of her soldier-son who has been
dead six years. But he does not stop her—she goes on and takes his
memory with her just as years ago she had taken the child's nightmare
back with her from the bedroom into the living room and into the circle
of lamplight, where "it had taken its place there like a ghost" (p. 347).
The mother's anguish over death is not defeat but persistence in the
belief that one can go on although life may be only an illusion, a drama
at the end of which there is nothing:

> But softly without a sound the dark curtain has rolled down. There is
> no more to come. That is the end of the play. But it's cold, it's still.
> There is nothing to be gained by waiting.
>
> "I can't bear it!" She sits up breathing the words and tosses the dark
> rug away. It is colder than ever, and now dusk is falling like an ash on
> the pallid water.
>
> And the little steamer growing determined, throbbed on, pressed on,
> as if at the end of the journey there waited. . . . ("Six Years After,"
> pp. 347-348.)

The changing function of the boat image parallels the change in Reality
from death, destruction, and darkness to life, beauty, and light.[6] In the
New Zealand short stories preceding and including "At the Bay," the
boat image functions as a symbol of escape, whereas in the stories written
after "At the Bay," the boat image functions as a symbol of triumph over
the fear of death in the journey through life. In "Prelude," Linda sees
the aloe as a ship of escape from life and time (pp. 92-93). In "At the
Bay," Linda sits in a "steamer" chair and dreams of the river boats in
China in which she escapes time with her father (p. 115). In the same
story, Jonathan Trout wants to escape. "I could cut off to sea . . ." (p.
130). But he knows he cannot escape because he is a ship without an
"anchor" (p. 131). In "The Stranger," the ship bringing Janey home is
stopped by death—the thing which makes escape impossible. By contrast,
the ship in "Six Years After," is not stopped by the presence of death but

rather grows determined and throbs on in the face of death (p. 348). In "The Voyage," the little girl, Fenella Crane, and her grandmother make the journey in the Picton boat, through the darkness of night after Fenella's mother has died, and safely return home. Although this story was completed August 14, 1921, and therefore predates "At the Bay" by one month, the boat image is a symbol of triumph over darkness and death because it is associated with the little girl and grandmother, the two characters who are favored with the ability to accept death. The character of the mother is dispensed with in this story:

> We resist, we are terribly frightened, the little boat enters the dark fearful gulf and our only cry is to escape—"put me on land again." But it's useless. Nobody listens. The shadowy figure rows on. One ought to sit still and uncover one's eyes.[7]

Notes

1. See note 3, Chapter I.
2. The difference between the reality in "At the Bay" and in "The Garden Party" parallels a change in Katherine Mansfield's attitude toward death, corruption, and suffering. The problem of how the ugliness and intolerable corruption of life could be borne (see Notes to Chapter III, n. 3) was resolved finally by her belief that it must be accepted. In her *Journal* for December 19, 1920 (p. 228), she wrote:

   > There is no limit to human suffering. When one thinks: Now I have touched the bottom of the sea—now I can go no deeper, one goes deeper. And so it is for ever. I thought last year in Italy: Any shadow more would be death. But this year has been so much more terrible that I think with affection of the Casetta! Suffering is boundless, it is eternity. One pang is eternal torment. Physical suffering is child's play. To have one's breast crushed by a great stone—one could laugh!

   > I don't want to die without leaving a record of my belief that suffering can be overcome. For I do believe it. What must one do? There is no question of what Jack (her husband, John Middleton Murry) calls "passing beyond it". This is false.

   > One must *submit*. Do not resist. Take it. Be overwhelmed. Accept it fully. Make it *part of life*.

   > Everything in life that we really accept undergoes a change. So suffering must become Love. This is the mystery. This is what I must do.

3. The hat as a symbol of Mrs. Sheridan's world which is blind to the reality of death is discussed in Chapter III.
4. Not only must corruption be accepted, but it must be transmuted into Beauty.

   > But do you really feel (she wrote to the Honorable Dorothy Brett, March 9, 1922) all beauty is marred by ugliness and the lovely woman has bad teeth? I don't feel quite that. For it seems to me if Beauty were Absolute it would no longer be the kind of Beauty it is. Beauty triumphs over ugliness in Life. That's what I feel. And that marvellous triumph is what I long

to express. The poor man lives and the tears glitter in his beard and that is so beautiful one could bow down. Why? Nobody can say. I sit in a waiting-room where all is ugly, where it's dirty, dull, dreadful, where sick people waiting with me to see the doctor are all marked by suffering and sorrow. And a very poor workman comes in, takes off his cap humbly, beautifully, walks in tiptoe, has a look as though he were in Church, has a look as though he believed that behind that doctor's door there shone the miracle of *healing*. And all is changed, all is marvellous. It's only then that one sees for the first time what is happening. No, I don't believe in your frowsty housemaids, really. Life is, all at one and the same time, far more mysterious and far simpler than we know. It's like religion in that. If we want to have faith, and without faith we die, we must *learn to accept*. (*Letters*, pp. 452-453.)

About what she wanted to convey in "The Garden Party" Katherine Mansfield wrote to William Gerhardi, March 13, 1922:

The diversity of life and how we try to fit in everything, Death included. That is bewildering for a person of Laura's age. She feels things ought to happen differently. First one and then another. But life isn't like that. We haven't the ordering of it. Laura says, "But all these things must not happen at once." And Life answers, "Why not? How are they divided from each other?" And they do all happen, it is inevitable. And it seems to me there is beauty in that inevitability. (*Letters*, p, 454.)

5. In Katherine Mansfield's estimation, accepting darkness and light together was the most profound human experience. Praising Dostoevsky for this in a letter to John Middleton Murry, dated November 4, 1917, she described him as "a being who Loved, in spite of everything adored LIFE even while he knew the dark, dark places" (*Letters*, p. 244).
6. Celeste T. Wright, "Katherine Mansfield's Boat Image," *Twentieth Century Literature*, I, 128-132 (October, 1955). Mrs. Wright is particularly interested in the relationship between Katherine Mansfield's life and her work, and she traces parallel use of the boat image in the short stories as well as in all of Katherine Mansfield's writings.
7. *Letters*, Oct. 1920, p. 334.

Chapter V

℘℘℘

The Critical Appraisal 1957-1997

New Zealand

P erhaps the most important occurrence in Mansfield scholarship was
the purchase of Mansfield's manuscripts and letters in 1958 by the
Government of New Zealand for deposit in the Turnbull Library at Victoria
University in Wellington. They were purchased at auction from the
estate of John Middleton Murry, Katherine Mansfield's husband, who
died in 1957. From 1959, the year of the acquisition of Mansfield's
manuscripts and letters by Victoria University at Wellington, much,
although not all, substantial scholarship has been done by New Zealanders
whereas previously it had been done largely by English and American
Scholars. In his 1959 article, "The Editing of Katherine Mansfield's
Journal and Scrapbook" (1959:62-69) Ian A. Gordon analyzed and
described the contents of the manuscript collection. In addition to much
miscellaneous writing, he found the original manuscripts of *The Journal*
and *The Scrapbook* and was able to describe the editing and synthesizing
done by Murry to produce the published versions.[1] An analytical catalog
of these manuscripts was prepared and published in "The Unpublished
Manuscripts of Katherine Mansfield", transcribed and edited by Margaret

Scott in the *Turnbull Library Record* Vols. 3-7 and 12 from 1970 through 1979. The process of preparing this catalog is described by Scott in her article, "The Extant Manuscripts of Katherine Mansfield" in *Etudes Anglaises* 26:4, 1973:413-419.

At the time of Mansfield's death on 9 January 1923, three collections of her short stories had been published: *In A German Pension* in 1911, *Bliss* in 1920, and *The Garden Party* in 1922. *Prelude* had been separately published in 1918 at the Hogarth Press by Leonard and Virginia Woolf. Shortly after Mansfield's death, two collections of short stories and a collection of poems, under the editorship of Murry were published: *The Dove's Nest* in 1923, *Something Childish* in 1924, and *Poems* in 1923. In the years from 1927 to 1954, Murry edited and published much of the writing left by Mansfield including *The Journal* in 1927, *The Letters* in 1928 in two volumes, *Letters* in 1929 in one volume including the letters to Murry, *The Aloe* in 1930, *Novels and Novelists* in 1930 (a collection of book reviews previously published during 1919 and 1920 in the journal, *The Athenaeum*, of which Murry was editor), *The Scrapbook* in 1937, *Collected Stories* (which included the stories in the five previously published collections), in 1945 and *The Journal, Definitive Edition*, in 1954.

A high point in Mansfield scholarship was the publication in 1974 by Longman, London, of *Undiscovered Country: The New Zealand Stories of Katherine Mansfield*, by Ian A. Gordon. This is the first time that Mansfield's New Zealand stories were collected and published in one anthology. In his introduction, Gordon quoted Mansfield extensively from letters and journal entries regarding why she turned her attention to New Zealand and what her creative purpose was in writing about the dominion in which she was born and the life she knew there, before she left forever in July 1908. It was through her later New Zealand stories that she both paid her 'sacred' debt to her 'undiscovered country' and established her reputation as a short story innovator of major stature. This anthology of New Zealand stories allows the reader to see what a novel by Mansfield might have been like had she written one.

> Many of her New Zealand short stories also fall into two cycles: one, the larger, about the Burnell family, the second about the Sheridans. KM seems to have been able to sustain interest, and the reader's in these characters. Indeed the stories most critics regard as her finest are from these two groups. Professor Ian Gordon's "Undiscovered Country" fits these stories together with other stories and journal entries

in such a way as to suggest what a novel based on these might have been like. (Boddy:1988, 154)

Before Katherine Mansfield departed from New Zealand, she went on a camping trip in with a group of people into the Urewera Wilderness of the North Island in November and December 1907. The notebook in which she kept an account of the trip was published for the first time in its entirety as *The Urewera Notebook* edited with an introduction by Ian A. Gordon in 1978. Although pages 22-33 of Murry's edition of the 1954 definitive Journal contains excerpts from the *Urewera Notebook*, Gordon takes Murry to task for misreadings, excisions, and suppressions of some of the material. Mansfield used the notes from her wilderness trip as a source for a number of her New Zealand stories. Rhoda Nathan in her critical study, *Katherine Mansfield*, 1988: p113-124, analyzes in detail the original background sources for "The Women at the Store" and other early New Zealand stories in *The Urewara Notebook*.

The 1980's witnessed the publication of entirely new editions of much of Katherine Mansfield's writing. *The Collected Letters* of Katherine Mansfield: Volume I 1903-1917, Volume II 1918-1919, Volume III 1919-1920, and Volume IV 1920-1921, were edited by Vincent O'Sullivan and Margaret Scott and published in 1984, 1987, 1993 and 1996 respectively. *The Aloe, with Prelude,* edited with an introduction by Vincent O'Sullivan appeared in 1982. *The Stories of Katherine Mansfield, Definitive Edition*, edited by Antony Alpers was published in 1984. And in 1987, *The Critical Writings of Katherine Mansfield,* edited with an introduction by Clare Hanson was published. Finally, *Poems of Katherine Mansfield*, edited by O'Sullivan and *Letters between Katherine Mansfield and John Middleton Murry* edited by Cherry Hankin appeared in 1988. "Mansfield's work, as a major innovator in the art of the short story, and as an indispensable part of the development of modernism was now beyond question." (Pilditch: 1996, p. xxx)

Perhaps the major theme that all Mansfield scholars and critics find in her stories, journals and letters is the experience of exile, expatriation or isolation. She felt herself to be an outsider, and she wrote about outsiders. British V. S. Pritchett in 1946, writing about "At the Bay" asked, "Who are these people?" and Alpers the New Zealander in 1953 responded that "At The Bay" is the colonial experience par excellence (where the Burnell family feels compelled to take another family with them for company.)[2] Kaplan commented:

I was surprised to discover her absence from *Women's Writing in Exile,* edited by Mary Lynn Broe and Angela Ingram (Chapel Hill: University of North Carolina Press, 1989) which considers a large number of other female modernists such as H. D., Rhys, Stein, and Barnes in terms of the experience of exile or expatriation, a subject about which Mansfield knew as much as anyone. (Kaplan: 1991, p. 2, note 5)

In New Zealand, Mansfield felt exiled from England by the colonial experience. In England, she felt exiled from her family in New Zealand. She also felt exiled from ordinary life by her illness,[3] and as a woman she was an exile among male writers. "Her loneliness and estrangements were personal, social, cultural, and national" (Gindin: 1996, p.217). Characters in her stories set in England or on the Continent, such as Rosabel, Ma Parker or the Little Governess, are most often solitary outsiders. Characters in her New Zealand stories, including members of the same family, are isolated from each other.

Commenting on the isolation of John Hammond, the husband in "The Stranger," Heather Murry notes, "Hammond expresses the terrible feeling of existential loneliness at the heart of all Katherine Mansfield's fiction" (Murray: 1990, p. 118). Murray also noted "the idea of the individual isolated irrevocably was one she held all her life . . ." (Murray: 1990, 40). Tomalin commented "The particular stamp of her fiction is also the isolation in which each character dwells" (Tomalin, 1987, p.6) while Hankin observed that "The loneliness and emotional apartness which separates one human being from another is in some way central to virtually every story she wrote" (Hankin: 1983, 222). This isolation of individual characters is analyzed and examined in The New Zealand stories in detail in Chapter One. Kaplan points out that although Mansfield was attracted to the sense of security she noted in the lives of Virginia Woolf and other members of Bloomsbury, she always remained an outsider to a considerable extent and that her satirical portraits of well-to-do-pseudo-bohemians all reflect her persistent awareness of exclusion. Kaplan also points out that Mansfield's colonial background gave her no prestige among the English intellectuals or among the academic and artistic establishment, and that her background was tainted with "money" and "trade" while her revolt against it left her without money and without "connections" (Kaplan: 1991, 12-13).

Characters in Mansfield's short stories experience a deep sense of uprootedness and even members of the same family in the New Zealand stories are isolated each from the other.

> . . . Katherine Mansfield started as a colonial and concluded as a Modernist, and . . . exemplified . . . rejection of the center, rejection of the borders as well, the sense of discomposure *everywhere*, the play of feeling present and absent at the same time in almost anyplace. (O'Sullivan: 1994, 13)

Modernism

A huge expansion in the number of quarterly and weekly magazines in England by the 1890's created opportunities for the publication of short stories. Two entirely different types of short stories flourished at the close of the nineteenth century. The first was the story with a definite plot, the descendant of the Gothic tale, and the second was the "plotless" story which concentrated on inner mood and impression rather than external event. The plotless story was especially associated with *The Yellow Book*, the famous 'little magazine' of the nineties.

The plotless story seems to arise naturally from the intellectual climate of the time. Friederich Nietzsche, the German philosopher had declared that God was dead, and Charles Darwin's theory of Evolution had produced a deep sense of man's insignificance in a changing universe. The only alternative to this world seemed to be to the retreat within, to the compensating powers of the imagination. With this retreat came emphasis on the significant moment which would be called 'epiphany' by later writers such as James Joyce—the moment of insight which is outside space and time, revealed only fleetingly to the imagination, but redeeming human existence in time.

Katherine Mansfield modeled her early stories on those of the *Yellow Book* writers. Internal crises replaced the external crisis of plot. Mansfield used the epiphany as the focal point of her stories. From the *Yellow Book* writers she would have learned the techniques of stylized interior monologue, flashback, and daydream, which became very important in her work. She probably did not learn these techniques from Anton Chekhov, whom she admired greatly, because by 1909, when she probably first read Chekhov, his techniques by comparison would have seemed old-fashioned. Elizabeth Bowen was probably the first to point out that Mansfield was the first writer to see in the short story the ideal reflector of the day.

Although Mansfield's talents were peculiarly suited to the short story, she did try on at least three occasions to write a novel. These were *Juliet* in 1906, *Maata* from 1908 to 1915, and *Karori* as late as 1921-22. The latter was to include "Prelude" and "At the Bay" and to be based on the Burnell family. In addition to the Burnell family stories, she planned a cycle to be based on the Sheridan family and to include "The Garden Party" and "Her First Ball." It would appear that Mansfield herself did not separate the short story and novel form as absolutely as modern genre conscious critics have done. Towards the end of her career she seems to have been developing the story cycle form. Perhaps she viewed the cycle of stories as a bridge between the short story and the novel, as for example "Dubliners" by James Joyce or "Go Down Moses" by William Faulkner.

The main influences on Mansfield's work up to 1908 when she left New Zealand for the second and last time was symbolism through the writings of Arthur Symons and Oscar Wilde. From both she took ideas about aesthetic theory which continually influenced her art. One such influence was the Symbolist belief that things should not be conveyed through descriptive analysis, but evoked through concrete images and symbols. Almost every detail in a Mansfield story has a symbolic as well as a narrative function. Details or images work together to create a mood or evolve a theme which is never directly stated. She was also influenced by the Symbolist belief in the organic unity of the perfect work of art, which meant for Mansfield that form and content were indissolubly united. Although the work of art could be considered analogous to natural organic life, it was also, paradoxically, outside organic life, outside reality with its own laws and nature. In her journal of November 26, 1921, Mansfield wrote:

> Reality cannot become the idea, the dream, and it is not the business of the artist to grind an axe, to try to impose his vision of life upon the existing world. Art is not an attempt of the artist to reconcile existence with his vision: it is an attempt of the artist to create his own world *in* this world. That which suggests the subject to the artist is the *unlikeness* to what we accept as reality. We single out—we bring into the light— we put up higher.

The symbolist writers, including Walter Pater, attempted to convey meaning through the physical properties of language and sound sense. They used the musical analogy for prose to signify an ideal of nondiscursive expressiveness and this is an image used by Mansfield, in a letter to Richard Murry January 17, 1921, for what she was trying to do in prose. ". . . after I'd written it [Miss Brill] I read it aloud—numbers of times— just as one would play over a musical composition—trying to get it nearer and nearer to the expression—until it fitted her" (*Letters*, 1932: 360-61).

Modernism is the term generally used for the avant garde literature published in Europe and the United States between World War I and World War II. A broad definition includes a combination of the following: revolt against Victorian fathers, recognition of the artist's alienation, pursuit of the contemporary in language, psychology and behavior, and creation of dynamic original forms in which to contain a newly awakened sense of present reality. Although in 1934, T. S. Eliot selected Mansfield's story "Bliss" as an illustration of the dominant experimental tendency of contemporary fiction, Mansfield is excluded from the burgeoning number of studies recently published on the evolution of Modernism. Surprisingly, she is given very limited attention in Gilbert and Gubar's *No Man's Land: The Place of the Woman Writer in the Twentieth Century* (1988) and only passing notice in their *The Female Imagination and the Modernist Aesthetic* (1986). Sydney Janet Kaplan states that traditional definitions of modernism are flawed because they cancel out the significant efforts of women and that women are at the center of British Modernism. Many of the most revolutionary innovations employed in Mansfield's short fiction, including the plotless story, use of stream of consciousness, and emphasis on the psychological moment occurred even earlier than they did in the works of her contemporaries, including Virginia Woolf.

By the end of the 1970's, the Alpers and the Meyers biographies had appeared followed by Hankin, 1983, Fullbrook, 1986 and Tomalin, 1988, all of which provide scholarly evidence of the links between Mansfield's life and work. The single most extensive study of Mansfield's participation in the movement of literary modernism is Sydney Janet Kaplan's *Katherine Mansfield and the Origins of Modernist Fiction* (1991). It is Kaplan's view that the women at the center of British Modernism were attempting to discover new methods for conveying women's reality. Kaplan relates Mansfield's intellectual and sexual development to changes in women's expectations and roles in the early twentieth century. Kaplan explores the link between experimentation and the need to express a definite sense of women's reality which their inherited masculine culture would neither accept nor allow. It was this effort of British Modernist women writers to communicate experiences and feelings that went either unnoticed or was trivialized. Although Modernism changed gradually over time, Mansfield's development shows many of the features of early modernism. Both T. S. Eliot's "Wasteland" and James Joyce's *Ulysses* were published in 1922. This English modernism of the early 1920's also had an effective doctrine to explain and justify that body of work for which T. S. Eliot was largely responsible. But the submerged voice in this formulation, according to Kaplan, is female which achieves its decisive formulation in the mid to late 1920's with the masterpieces *Pilgrimage*, "Prelude," and *To the Light House*. In addition, there was the rhetorically effective doctrine for which Virginia Woolf is largely responsible that explains and justifies the masterpieces. Woolf's *"A Room of One's Own"* is considered the first modern text of feminist criticism. Kaplan goes on to point out that some influences are the same—Pater, Symons, Bergson, the James Brothers—while others have a greater influence on women: George Eliot, the Brontes, Olive Schreiner, and *The Yellow Book*. Kaplan also points out that, instead of Ford, Hulme, Pound, and Eliot, we have May Sinclair, Dorothy Richardson, Katherine Mansfield, and Virginia Woolf. Kaplan states that this disparity conforms to Elaine Showalter's description of how "women's culture forms a collective experience within the cultural whole" or is a muted group alongside the dominant group (1991: 9). Female modernists saw their inheritance as coming from both their fathers and mothers while male modernists acknowledged only inheritance from the fathers. To male modernists, the mother, not the father, is what must be escaped from. Kaplan points out that Modernism from the female line is fuller, more complex, and more relevant to contemporary readers and that any analysis of Mansfield's significance "must be grounded in theoretical considerations of gender and responsive to the questions of the meaning of sexuality itself in her writings" (Kaplan 1991:9). Mansfield developed techniques that allowed her to probe feminine consciousness before either Virginia Woolf or Dorothy Richardson. Only Gertrude Stein was writing experimental fiction before Katherine Mansfield. "The Tiredness of Rosabel" written by Mansfield in 1908 employs the stream of consciousness technique, and this earliest story told from within is an attempt to describe a woman's consciousness.

Katherine Mansfield and Virginia Woolf shared a great deal as contemporary British Modernists, but they also shared significant differences in terms of experience, education, and class. Significantly, Mansfield attended Queens College, London (1903-1906) and was introduced in literature classes to late 19th century avant garde literature. Virginia Woolf, on the other hand, was educated by governesses, and although she read extensively in her father's impressive library, she never attended formal school. Virginia Woolf, as the daughter of Leslie Stephen, had to overthrow the full weight of the phallocentric intellectual tradition that Stephen represented. For Katherine Mansfield, art was a away to reject her father's materialist values. She did not have to also reject his intellectual values. For an extended analysis of differences and similarities between Mansfield and Woolf and their writings see Kaplan (1991) p. 12-16, Tomalin (1988) p. 198-203, and McLaughlin (1983) p. 152-161. Although one can find in her fiction a feminist critique of women's historical situation, she did not connect her understanding of alienation and victimization with either a Marxist or feminist political analysis. Woolf did not do so either until years after Mansfield's death. Mansfield died too early and after undergoing too much personal suffering. She linked her own suffering to human suffering, and did not articulate her social critique of human suffering in recognizably political terms. Mansfield was a Modernist in late adolescence and by her early twenties her style was refined and perfected, reflecting a merging of experimental techniques with feminist insight.

Discarding conventional plot structure, Mansfield began her stories *in medias res* and usually ended before the climax, because she felt that the introduction and neatly concluded ending conveyed an artificial or distorted sense of life. No stage is set, no background is given, the reader is plunked down immediately into the action. To penetrate the exterior of conventional behavior and present inner experience, she relied on the dramatic monologue technique. She used the stream of consciousness technique as a way to get into the character's mind or psyche. This enabled her to present various time levels with great economy. Through the daydream and formal flashbacks she was able to present the past, present, and inner world as well as multiple points of view.

> As her stories affirm over and over, reality is disclosed in how minds converge, drift apart, lose touch, come back—like the backgammon pegs as Beryl and Stanley play their game in "Prelude". It is found in images constantly on the point of becoming memory (O'Sullivan: 1994, 18).

Objectivity or truth was always her aim. "At the end *truth* is the only thing *worth having*"[4] To this end, the device of the story narrator was discarded and the authorial point of view dispensed with. To present the greatest "truth" of an object or character, it must be recreated, not just discoursed upon. The author becomes the object in a momentary vision:

> When I write about ducks I swear that I am a white duck. . . . Then follows the moment when you are *more* duck, *more* apple, or *more* Natasha than any of these objects could ever possibly be, and so you create them anew.[5]

About writing "The Stranger" she said: "It isn't as though one sits and watches the spectacle. That would be thrilling enough, God knows. But one is the spectacle for a time."[6]

But the universality of truth which she wished to convey must be done indirectly. Speaking of the "tragic knowledge" gained by the experience of World War I, she wrote in a letter to John Middleton Murry:

> But, of course, you don't imagine I mean by this knowledge let-us-eat-and-drinkism. No, I mean "deserts of vast eternity." But the difference is I couldn't tell anybody bang out about those deserts: they are my secret. I might write about a boy eating strawberries or a woman combing her hair on a windy morning, and that is the only way I can ever mention them. But they *must* be there.[7]

To present truth obliquely was her greatest problem: "But how are we going to convey these overtones, half tones, quarter tones, these hesitations, doubts, beginnings, if we go at them *directly*?"[8] The tangential approach to her material allowed for the maximum of implication. William York Tindall likened her method to that of the symbolist poets: "She often worked by indirection, allowing overtones, hints, and silences to suggest more than the situation seems to hold."[9] By repeatedly focusing on a minute detail, ostensibly trivial emotion or fragmented occurrence, she was able by suggestion to work out to some intensity of feeling or universality of meaning about the major forces of life. David Daiches analyzes her method:

She starts with one particular, and such universal aspects as there are emerge very indirectly by implication, as a result of her organization of detail. . . . In this type of literature it is the actual form of the story which gives symbolic (universal) value to the incidents. There is no simple relation between form and content, no story x presented through medium y. . . . It is like lyric poetry, a type of writing where conception unites simultaneously subject (matter) with style (form).[10]

Katherine Mansfield wrote poetry throughout her life, and it is her poetic sensibility that canonizes her short stories in English modernism; her 'special prose,' which incorporated the influences of the Romantic poets, the aesthetes, including Pater and Wilde, brought to the short story a new fluidity and intensity. Her use of impressionism, lyric compression, symbols, images, multiple and shifting perspectives, and juxtaposed scenes enabled her to become an innovator in narrative form. These qualities are reflected in the stories she wrote from 1916 to 1923 and can best be seen in a comparison between "The Aloe" written in 1916 and revised as "Prelude" in 1917.[11] The stories she wrote in the period from 1912 to 1915 reflected her technical experimentation for greater objectivity, while those she wrote from 1908 to 1911 are what she called her "cries against corruption."

Not only did Mansfield use an oblique approach to her material in building up intensity to the significant point she wished to convey, but because the story ends just before the climax, the climax takes place within the reader. In this way demand was put upon the imagination or poetry-making faculty of the reader. This was in keeping with her desire to convey a sense of "mystery" or a sense of possibilities beyond what is actually stated.

From her stories, letters, and journal one can see that World War I was the single most important public event in Katherine Mansfield's lifetime. In addition to the death of her beloved brother at the front in 1915, many of her friends were also killed. For a civilian, Mansfield experienced a good deal of the war. She visited Francis Carco in the War Zone and was perhaps the first to record the effects of gassing after seeing its victims only a few days after gassing had been introduced. Then in 1918 she was under direct bombardment in Paris for those weeks that the Germans, using 'Big Bertha',. shelled the city every eighteen minutes. The experience of the War for Mansfield was the recognition that a world had gone, entirely and forever.

In a letter to John Middleton Murry, Mansfield criticized Virginia Woolf's *Night and Day* (1919) for its apparent lack of concern about the war. She disliked the novel, stating that:

> My private opinion is that it is a lie in the Soul. The war has never been: that is what the message is. I don't want (G. forbid!) mobilisation and the violation of Belgium, but the novel can't just leave the war out. . . . I feel in the profoundest sense that nothing can ever be the same—that, as artists, we are traitors if we feel otherwise: we have to take it into account and find new expressions, new moulds for our new thoughts and feelings. . . . We have to face our war.[12]

The war had brought permanent fragmentation to what living in Europe had meant. "Anything like reality was no longer to be looked for in the larger social and religious structures the war had undermined, from a past that no longer related to oneself." (O'Sullivan: 1994, 17).

Analyzing the relationship between World War I and Modernism, Booth reports that

> . . . Modernism has to believe that interior experience is at least as profound if not more profound than exterior experience, because otherwise the physical experience disappears with the physical body, and otherwise the implications generated by the physical experience of war have to be re-experienced physically in order to be understood. . . . Modernism thus tries to internalize the perceptual and imaginative repercussions of war—to transform them into imaginative material and always at the same time to point toward the battlefield, toward the physical experience of war. . . (Booth: 1996, 162).

Booth goes on to point out, as an example, the fear that Kezia has in "Prelude," looking from the window of the empty house, which is closely associated with the physical act of perception. Kezia's awareness of the materiality of the glass provides a physical analog for the act of perception that then takes on a life of its own in the character of IT. "Mansfield's characters inhabit worlds that are perceptually threatening to come alive, in part because the boundary between literal and metaphysical is shifty." (Booth: 1996, 160-61).

Feminism

Feminist criticism is loosely described as

> Any of a variety of approaches to literary criticism that attempt to examine the ways in which literature has been shaped according to issues of gender.

> Feminist literary theory originated largely in the women's movement that followed World War II. Two of the earliest documents of feminist theory are Simone de Beauvoir's book *Le Deuxieme Sexe* (1949; *The Second Sex*) and Kate Millett's *Sexual Politics* (1970). Feminist criticism established several aims: to critique the established canon of Western literature and to expose the standards on which it is based as patriarchal; to recover forgotten and neglected texts by women in order to reevaluate them; to establish "gynocriticism," the study of woman-centered writing, and to establish a women's canon; and to explore the cultural construction of gender and identity.[13]

Claire Hanson in her introduction to *The Gender of Modernism*, edited by Scott, as well as in her introduction to *The Critical Writings of Katherine Mansfield*, edited by Hanson, notes that Mansfield is often compared with the women painters Berthe Morisot and Mary Cassatt because their works deal with the domestic aspects of life. Although Hanson goes on to make a case for Mansfield's being a great writer, she comments on the fact that, especially in the past, Mansfield's work has frequently been compared with writers and artists who have represented a world of women, their activities, and their relationships.

By examining Mansfield's attitude toward women, toward female subjectivity, and toward questions of female expression, Susan Pratt suggests that Mansfield's stories do write a feminine world. Pratt focuses attention on Mansfield's domestic settings, her preference for indeterminate endings and themes, her fascination for problems of expression, and her willingness to leave ideas unarticulated.

Elaine Showalter in *A Literature of Their Own: British Women Novelists from Bronte to Lessing*, classifies Mansfield as one of a group of feminist writers born between the years 1880 and 1900, who "In their rejection of male society and masculine culture . . . retreated more and more toward a separatist literature of inner space" (1977: 33). Not only do Linda in "Prelude" and "At the Bay" and Janey Hammond in "The

Stranger" frequently retreat into a private world to protect themselves from their husbands, but all the women in the house in "At the Bay" feel great relief when Stanley leaves for work.

'Good-bye, Stanley,' called Beryl, sweetly and gaily. It was easy enough to say good-bye! And there she stood, idle, shading her eyes with her hand. The worst of it was Stanley had to shout good-bye too, for the sake of appearances. Then he saw her turn, give a little skip and run back to the house.

She was glad to be rid of him!

Yes, she was thankful. Into the living-room she ran and called 'He's gone!' Linda cried from her room:

'Beryl! Has Stanley gone?' Old Mrs. Fairfield appeared, carrying the boy in his little flannel coatee.

'Gone?'

'Gone!'

Oh, the relief, the difference it made to have the man out of the house.

Their very voices changed as they called to one another; they sounded warm and loving and as if they shared a secret. Beryl went over to the table. 'Have another cup of tea, mother. It's still hot.' She wanted, somehow, to celebrate the fact that they could do what they liked now. There was no man to disturb them; the whole perfect day was theirs.

'No, thank you, child,' said old Mrs. Fairfield, but the way at that moment she tossed the boy up and said 'a-goos-agoos-aga!' to him meant that she felt the same. The little girls ran into the paddock like chickens let out of a coop.

Even Alice, the servant girl, washing up the dishes in the kitchen, caught the infection and used the precious tank water in a perfectly reckless fashion.

'Oh, these men!' said she, and she plunged the teapot into the bowl and held it under the water even after it had stopped bubbling, as if it too was a man and drowning was too good for them. (1956: 106-107)

Stanley's departure for work brings a shared moment of relief and expressed liberation to all the women in the house.

As discussed in Chapter One, direct communication between characters in Katherine Mansfield's stories is almost non-existent. The one exception is the meeting between Linda and her brother-in-law, Jonathan Trout, in "At the Bay" where he tells Linda how much he hates his job, which he sees as a prison that keeps him from the larger world which he sees as a "vast, dangerous garden, waiting out there, undiscovered, unexplored." When Linda asks if it is not too late to change, Jonathan complains that it is too late and that he is old. As he bows his head, Linda notices the gray in his hair. They bow together before knowledge of immortality and in recognition of the inevitability of death.

Kate Fullbrook in *Katherine Mansfield*, the only avowedly feminist study of Mansfield, comments that:

> Image and plot, symbol and idea—all the elements of her fiction function as protests against any ideology of fixture and certainty. Katherine Mansfield's general commentary on her age is couched in her exposition of, her imaging of, contemporary women's consciousness, and in a prose attuned to catch the form of that experience. She implicitly demands the right to see women and their lives as the particulars from which the general historical situation can be deduced. But her fiction goes beyond an attempt to reflect the age in which she lived; it is a body of work that incites to revolt through its critical appraisal of the circumstances Katherine Mansfield sees and records (Fullbrook, 1986; 128).

All Mansfield critics agree that Linda Burnell is a reluctant mother who does not love her children and who is overly dependent on the mothering provided by her own mother, Mrs. Fairfield. Mary Burgan thinks that Linda accepts childbirth looking at the aloe plant which grows in front of the new house in "Prelude." Just as all plants must flower, so "Linda Burnell thus comes to a limited recognition that childbirth is inevitable by linking herself with the process of nature which the aloe symbolizes" (Burgan, 1978: 406).

When Kezia asks her mother if the aloe ever flowers, Linda answers with a smile and half shut eyes, "Yes. . . . Once every hundred years." The unseeing smile and brief answer separates Linda from her daughter. She seems barely to respond to the child's need for some understanding of the mysteries of birth and time symbolized by the aloe plant. Without more positive assurance than Linda's smile, Kezia will be left alone with her anxiety. Her life as a woman will be beset by the threatening phallic presence with its blind stem.

Later, in "Prelude," Linda stands before the aloe plant again, this time with her mother, Mrs. Fairfield. Now the plant presents her with an image of freedom. Linda thinks of the aloe as a ship that might take her miles away and protect her from Stanley. Although she cannot give herself generously to her children, her recognition of her biological fate saves her from the near insanity of her morning dreams. Unlike Linda, Mrs. Fairfield does not need to search out some idea of eternity to justify her existence. Linda's acceptance of the aloe in "Prelude" marks a temporary relief from her hysterical rebellion, and in "At the Bay," her final release is depicted.

The baby that Linda is expecting in "Prelude" has been born in "At the Bay." Sitting on the lawn with her new son, Linda turns to the baby and says, "Hallo, my funny." In light of the boys right to be, Linda has made the necessary accommodation with nature in the form of her son, and that accommodation renews her capacity for more general sympathy. It is shortly after this that Linda has her encounter with Jonathan. The world of nature has changed for her on the day she accepts her son.

In Mansfield's short stories, the woman's acceptance of sex and reproduction is never simple or easy. But there is a clear sense that the alternative is a flirtation with the temptations of the inhuman. In the final section of "At the Bay" Linda's sister Beryl flees from Harry Kember and in so doing rejects the sterility of perverse womanhood. Mansfield seems to see her artistic as well as maternal creativity to be linked in some way with the family relationships of her childhood. Her re-enactments of the history of her family give the rejected child the opportunity to rejoice "that a man is born into the world." This is the promise she made when her beloved brother was killed in 1915 during World War I that her 'sacred' debt was to make him and their undiscovered country live forever. The acceptance of the baby implies the acceptance of death as well as birth. Birth becomes then, not just a matter of the individual woman's physical pain. The acceptance or rejection of it rules the lives of her children, making them capable or incapable of their own creativity.

As an artist, taking a role parallel to her mother's fecundity, Mansfield finds a way to create anew or to give a new birth to her mother's children.

It helped to free her from the bonds of the past to a vision of a future that could accept illness, anxiety, sexual disparities, and the facts of death. As Mary Burgan notes, "Mothers and their daughters are inevitable rivals, but they must overcome this rivalry if the younger woman is to accept her own role in the cycle of life later." (Burgan, 1978: 405).

In the modernist period women did produce recognizable Kunstlerroman. They shaped the conventions of this genre to their own purposes, and in the process of shifting perspective they produced uniquely female images of creativity. Up to this time two polar attitudes toward female generativity—revulsion and revision—remained the axis on which female definitions of creativity hinged. Artistic production and biological reproduction are either contradictory models furnishing alternative scripts or they are analogous, parallel models.

Some independence from pregnancy, fostered by a decrease in birth rate, a decrease in infant/maternal mortality, and availability of improved birth control, allowed for the re-imagining of birth itself. In addition, World War I provided greater independence for women as at the same time increased educational opportunities. In Virginia Woolf's *Orlando*, published in 1928, Orlando becomes a woman in the eighteenth century, marries in the nineteenth century, and gives birth to a child in the twentieth century. As Mary Burgan has already pointed out, the stories of Katherine Mansfield reveal how one woman artist overcomes her revulsion against generativity. By coming to terms with the centrality of birth, " by reconciling her writing with her rearing, Mansfield calls into question the identification of artistry with autonomy" (Gubar: 1983, 27).

Mansfield's later short stories redefine creativity and thus provide a model for understanding how feminist modernists accommodated their own independence to the discontinuity and lack of independence that have traditionally characterized female culture, without portraying themselves as aberrations. The contradictions of production and reproduction can be seen portrayed by late nineteenth century writers such as Rebecca Harding Davis, Olive Schreiner, and Elizabeth Stuart Phelps Ward. It is in "Prelude" that Mansfield "redefines women's unique creativity inside the gap that separates life and art." (Gubar: 1983, 27). Mansfield's later stories typify the redefinition of women as creators in the artist novels of feminist modernists such as Dorothy Richardson, Willa Cather, and Virginia Woolf. This is quite different from Schreiner's *Story of an African Farm* (1883) which depicts the incompatible competition between artistic production and biological reproduction. In Ward's *Story of Avis* (1887), Avis like Edna Pontellier in Kate Chopin's *The Awakening*, (1899), is torn between her artistic impulse and the repetition of domestic labor. In Anais Nin's "Birth" (1938) the reader is told that "woman's creation must be exactly like her creation of children" (Gubar: 1983, 33).

Mansfield's "Prelude" is not only the story of the move of a family from one house to another; it is also a story about the move from imagining the womb as a store or cavity to "imagining the womb as the transformative matrix of primordial change" (Gubar: 1983, 34). The title of the story, "Prelude", implies not only a prelude to life in the new house, but a prelude to the birth of the brother. It is also a prelude to the process of composition that allows him to live again. In addition it can be seen as a prelude to a new history of the Great War, to a new appreciation of literary modernism and as a prelude to later Mansfield fiction.

The death of her brother in 1915 in World War I resulted in Mansfield recreating his birth in fiction. In this sense, she becomes her brother's mother. By bearing her brother in fiction, she comes to terms with her dread of mothering. "Her brother's death liberates her to celebrate women's capacity to birth as an aspect of the artistry she enacts as a fiction writer" (Gubar: 1983, 34). But as soon as her brother is born, Mansfield erases him and creates in the "undiscovered country" of their childhood, a nostalgic motherland made up of women who, in spite of their differences, "live together in a family that is sustained by their common artistry" (Gubar: 1983, 34). "Prelude" and "At the Bay" can be read as an anatomy of female development from girlhood (Kezia) to old age (Mrs. Fairfield). The aloe plant in "Prelude" is "repossessed by the women and redeemed—a symbol of female resistance, escape, and ecstasy" (Gubar: 1983, 37).

Gubar demonstrates that:

> the aloe speaks of the resiliency, endurance, and strength of women preserving the life of the family in spite of its terrible call on their powers of self preservation. The aloe symbolizes women's intimation of their own regenerative powers. The imaginative transformation of the aloe epitomizes the transformative character of the female imagination and related by Mansfield to the body that is entered, swollen, and scarred by childbearing (Gubar: 1983, 37).

"Prelude," "At the Bay," and "The Doll's House" dramatize three shifts in perspective that, Gubar demonstrates, allowed feminist modernists to reshape the Kunstlerroman in light of their own images of creativity: the shifts in perspective involve a revisionary domestic mythology, fantasies of a woman's language, and the transformation of matrophobia into matrisexuality, the erotics of mother and child (Gubar: 1983, 39). In "At the Bay" the definition between shore and water is blurred. Women inhabit this blurred area to represent the blurred boundaries between self and other. Mansfield implies that the merging identity experienced by mother and child constitutes an "erotic interdependence of the kind that Chodrow claims endows female subjectivity with greater complexity, greater plasticity, and great empathy" (Gubar: 1983, 45).

Virginia Woolf's novel *To the Lighthouse* (1927), in Gubar's view, demonstrates the revisionary domesticity that Mansfield celebrates. It dramatizes the coercion and cost of the mother's (Mrs. Ramsay's) script, the permeability of women's interiority, and the mother-daughter (Mrs. Ramsay and Lily Briscoe) eroticism, an eroticism that predates heterosexuality for women.

Patricia Moran, in "Unholy Meanings" (1991: 105-125), offers a somewhat different reading of the New Zealand stories. Noting that some critics read Mansfield's career as a straight development from an early repudiation of maternity in her first collection, *In A German Pension*, (1911) to a celebration of maternity as an analog for female artistry in her well known "Prelude" (1917) and "At the Bay" (1921), Moran suggests that this approach simplifies the contradictory aspects of her work, and in particular ignores the undeniably male-identified aspects of her biography.

> Mansfield's writing reveals one woman's hatred and rejection of her female body based on irrational fantasies of maternal power. . . . The metaphysical obsession with eating and engulfment pervading all of Mansfield's work, biographical and fictional suggest more generally how a problematic relation to the mother and the female body informs not only the literal experience of eating disorders, but also the issue of female creativity (Moran: 1991, 106).[14]

Moran suggests that images of eating can express the dilemma Jane Flax identifies as the female conflict between nurturance and autonomy, fusion and separation: to eat is to merge with the mother; to refuse food may express a desire for separation and autonomy. Moran reads Mansfield's work as saying that either a woman can be a mother or she can be a writer and that the materiality of the female body somehow overwhelms female subjectivity, and makes her unable to create. For Moran it is Linda's refusal to assume or accept a maternal role that permits her daughter Kezia both to consider alternative modes of female activity and to separate from the seductive figure of the grandmother, Mrs. Fairfield (Moran: 1991, 121). Moran offers the reading that Mansfield never resolved her conflict with the pre-oedipal mother within.

According to Ellen Moers, an important shift occurred in fiction written by women in the 1920's in both Europe and the United States. Moers suggests that there was a movement from the heterosexual plot of courtship, marriage, and adultery to the story of what she calls "maternal seduction" (Moers: 1977, 354). Virginia Woolf, Gertrude Stein, Willa Cather, and Colette, Moers points out, all recount the female artist's story in relation not to a father or male lover, but to a powerful, seductive, traditionally female mother-goddess. Analyzing this shift in women's fiction, Marianne Hirsch notes that Woolf and her contemporaries thematize the relation of the process of artistic production to familial configurations and psychological structures. Female Kunstlerroman of the 1920's, which differ radically from the family romances of the Victorian period, feature young and middle-aged women who renounce love and marriage in favor of creative work, and who renounce connection in favor of self-affirmation. The choice is intimately bound up in their relationships with their mothers but is often in great conflict with the choices the mothers themselves made. What emerges in the texts of Woolf and Colette of this period is an ambivalent preoccupation with the mother, which oscillates between a longing for connection and a need for disconnection.

Hirsch finds that the conjunction of the refusal of heterosexual love and the romance plot and of a celebration of mothers is a pervasive feature of women's writing in the 1920's. She notes that it is important to realize that this interrogation and celebration of maternity is in itself new for women writers and that this interest in maternity could only emerge at a time in history when motherhood had become less life threatening and more of a choice for women. It became possible for women to re-imagine the maternal.

> Significantly, however, they did so not for themselves but for the generation of their mothers, attempting to unite the disparate experiences of two generations separated by a remarkable shift in opportunity for women, to minimize the distance between the emergence of women and artists and the conventional femininity

embraced by their mothers. . . . Even while the daughter-artist herself still does not become a mother, the mother's life can be and needs to be known and explored in its details, incorporated into the daughter's vision. (Hirsch: 1989, 97).

Hirsch cites Gubar's analysis of Katherine Mansfield's liberation from the fear of maternity and her ability to envision a form of art centered not in autonomy but in connection, not in a bodiless mind, but in a female body, as having been a direct result of her brother's death in World War I. "Her brother's death liberates her to celebrate women's capacity to birth as an aspect of the artistry she enacts as a fiction writer" (Gubar: 1983, 34). Hirsch demonstrates that while claiming to bring the dead brother back to life, Mansfield, like Woolf and Colette, creates a fictional world in which women and female relationships flourish.

Notes

1. For a more extended article on Murry's editing of the Mansfield Journal see Waldron, Philip, "Katherine Mansfield's Journal" in *Twentieth Century Literature: A Scholarly and Critical Journal* 20 (1974): 11-18.
2. For a fuller discussion of Pritchett and Alpers comments on exile and isolation see Notes to Chapter One, note 1.
3. For an excellent discussion of the effect of Mansfield's illnesses on her writing see Burgan, Mary. *Illness, Gender, and Writing: The Case of Katherine Mansfield.* Baltimore, Johns Hopkins University Press, 1994.
4. Mansfield, Katherine. *Journal*, edited by John Middleton Murry, definitive edition. London: Constable 1954:185.
5. Mansfield, Katherine. *Letters*, edited by John Middleton Murry, special one volume edition. New York: Knopf, 1932. Oct. 11, 1917, p. 74.
6. Ibid., Nov. 10, 1919, p. 247.
7. Ibid., Nov. 16, 1919, p. 255.
8. Ibid., Jun. 24, 1922, p. 476.
9. Tindall: 1956: 207.
10. Daiches: 1937: p. 75-76.
11. See *The Aloe, with Prelude* edited with an introduction by Vincent O'Sullivan (1982) for a detailed, in-depth discussion of how Mansfield transformed *The Aloe* (1915) into *Prelude* (1917).
12. Letter to John Middleton Murry, 10 November 1919. See also Mansfield's review of Virginia Woolf's *Night and Day*, "A Ship Comes into the Harbour" in Novels and Novelists: 1930, 112-115.
13. *Merriam-Webster's Encyclopedia of Literature.* Springfield: Merriam Webster, 1995: 409.
14. Moran: 1991, 106. For a discussion of this female conflict, see also Flax, Jane, "The Conflict Between Nurturance and Autonomy in the Mother-Daughter Relationships and within Feminism," in *Feminist Studies* 4 (June 1978): 171-89.

Bibliography

Alpers, Antony. *Katherine Mansfield, a Biography*. New York: Knopf, 1953.
———. *The Life of Katherine Mansfield*. New York: Viking Press, 1980.
Beach, Joseph Warren. "Katherine Mansfield and Her Russian Master" in Virginia Quarterly Review, XXVII (Autumn 1951), 604-608.
Berkman, Sylvia. *Katherine Mansfield, a Critical Study*. New Haven: Yale University Press, 1951.
Bicker, Lyn. "Public and Private Choices: Public and Private Voices," in Goldman, Dorothy. *Women and World War I: The Written Response*. New York: St. Martin's Press, 1993. p. 92-112.
Boddy, Gillian. *Katherine Mansfield: The Woman and the Writer*. New York: Penguin Books, 1988.
Bogan, Louise. *Selected Criticism*. New York: Noonday, 1955.
Booth, Allyson. *Postcards from the Trenches: Negotiating the Space Between Modernism and the First World War*. New York: Oxford University Press, 1996.
Brewster, Dorothy and Angus Burrell. *Modern Fiction*. New York: Columbia University Press, 1934.
Brophy, Brigid. "Katherine Mansfield's Self-Depiction" in *Michigan Quarterly Review 5*. (Spring 1966) : 89-93. Reprinted in the *Critical Response to Katherine Mansfield*, edited by Jan Pilditch. Westport, CT and London: Greenwood Press, 1996. p. 89-94.
Burgan, Mary. "Childbirth Trauma in Katherine Mansfield's Early Stories" *Modern Fiction Studies*, 24:3, Autumn 1978, p. 395-412.
———. *Illness, Gender, and Writing: The Case of Katherine Mansfield*. Baltimore: Johns Hopkins University Press, 1994.
Carter, Susanne. *Mothers and Daughters in American Short Fiction: An Annotated Bibliography of Twentieth-Century Women's Literature* (Bibliographies and Indexes in Women's Studies, Number 19). Westport, CT and London: Greenwood Press, 1993.
Cather, Willa. "Katherine Mansfield" in *Not Under Forty*. New York: Knopf, 1936, pp. 123-147.
Citron, Pierre. "Katherine Mansfield et La France" in Revue de Literature Comparee, XX (April 1940), 173-193.
Clark, I. G. *Katherine Mansfield*. Wellington: Beltane, 1944.
Daiches, David. "Katherine Mansfield and the Search for Truth" in *The Novel and the Modern World*. Chicago: University of Chicago Press, 1939, pp. 67-79.
Daly, Saralyn, R. *Katherine Mansfield*. New York: Twayne Publishers, 1965.
Darling, Wanda. "Katherine Mansfield: Her Writing, Development, and Literary Effect." Unpublished master's thesis, Columbia University, 1941.

Delany, Paul. "Short and Simple Annals of the Poor: Katherine Mansfield's 'The Doll's House'" in *MOSAIC: A Journal for the Comparative Study of Literature and Ideas,* 10:1 (1976): 7-17

Dinkins, Paul. Review of *Letters of Katherine Mansfield to John Middleton Murry 1913-1922* in *Saturday Review,* XXXIV (October 20, 1951), 9.

———. "Katherine Mansfield: The Ending" in *Southwest Review,* XXXVIII (Summer 1953), 203-210.

Drummond, Wilhelmina. "A Psychosocial Study of Katherine Mansfield's Life," in *Early Child Development and Care,* (February 1990): 89-98

Flax, Jane. "The Conflict Between Nurturance and Autonomy in Mother-Daughter Relationships and within Feminism," in *Feminist Studies* 4 (June 1978): 171-89.

Fullbrook Kate. *Katherine Mansfield.* Bloomington: Indiana University Press, 1986.

Friis, Ann. *Katherine Mansfield: Life and Stories.* Copenhagen: Einar Munksgaard, 1946.

Garlington, Jack. "Katherine Mansfield: The Critical Trend" in *Twentieth Century Literature,* II (July 1956), 51-61.

———. "The Mating of Gwendolen: an Unattributed Short Story" in *Modern Language Notes,* LXXII (February 1956), 91-93.

Garlington, Jack O'Brien. "Literary Theory and Practice in the Short Stories of Katherine Mansfield." Unpublished Ph.D. dissertation, University of Wisconsin, 1954.

Gilbert, Sandra M. and Gubar, Susan. *The Female Imagination and the Modernist Aesthetic.* New York: Gordon and Breach Science Publishers, 1986.

———. and Gubar, Susan. *No Man's Land: The Place of the Woman Writer in the Twentieth Century.* New Haven: Yale University Press, 1988. 3 Vols.

Gindin, James. "Katherine Mansfield" in *Dictionary of Literary Biography.* V. 162. Detroit, Gale, 1996, p. 209-226.

Gordon, Ian. *Katherine Mansfield.* London: Longmans, Green, 1954.

Gordon, Ian A. "The Editing of Katherine Mansfield's Journal and Scrapbook" *Landfall,* XIII:I (March 1959), 62-69.

———. "Katherine Mansfield: The Wellington Years, a Reassessment" in *Critical Essays on Katherine Mansfield,* edited by Rhoda B. Nathan. New York: G.K. Hall, 1993. p. 61-74. Reprinted from *The Urerewa Notebook* by Katherine Mansfield, edited with an introduction by Ian A. Gordon. Oxford: Oxford University Press, 1978. p. 11-30.

Gordon, Ian Alistair. *Katherine Mansfield.* London, Published for the British Council by Longman Group Ltd., 1971.

Gubar, Susan. "The Birth of the Artist as Heroine: (Re) production, the Künstlerroman Tradition, and the Fiction of Katherine Mansfield" in Heilbrun, Carolyn G. and Margaret R. Higonnet, eds. *The Representation of Women in Fiction.* Baltimore and London, Johns Hopkins University Press, 1983. 19-59.

Hankin, Cherry A. *Katherine Mansfield and her Confessional Stories.* New York: St. Martin's Press, 1983.

Hanson, Clare, "Katherine Mansfield (1888-1923)" in *The Gender of Modernism: A Critical Anthology,* edited by Bonnie K. Scott. Bloomington: Indiana University Press, 1990. p. 298-315.

Head, Dominic. *The Modernist Short Story: A Study in Theory and Practice.* Cambridge [England], New York: Cambridge University Press, 1992.

Hirsch, Marianne. *The Mother/Daughter Plot: Narrative, Psychoanalysis, Feminism.* Bloomington: Indiana University Press, 1989.

Hoare, Dorothy. *Some Studies in the Modern Novel.* Philadelphia: Dufour, 1953.

Hynes, Sam. "The Defeat of the Personal" in *South Atlantic Quarterly,* LII (October 1953), 555-560.

Kaplan, Sydney Janet. *Feminine Conciousness in the Modern British Novel.* Urbana: University of Illinois Press, 1975.

———. *Katherine Mansfield and the Origins of Modernist Fiction.* Ithaca, Cornell University Press, 1991.

Kirkpatrick, B.J. *A Bibliography of Katherine Mansfield.* Oxford: Clarendon Press; New York: Oxford University Press, 1989.

Kobler, J.F. *Katherine Mansfield: A Study of the Short Fiction.* Boston: Twayne Publishers, 1990.

Kronenberger, Louis. Review of *Scrapbook* in *Nation,* CL (February 10, 1940), 217-219.

Lawlor, P. A. *Mansfieldiana,* Wellington: Beltane, 1948.

———. *The Mystery of Maata, a Katherine Mansfield Novel.* Wellington: Beltane, 1946.

McLaughlin, Ann L. "An Uneasy Sisterhood: Virginia Woolf and Katherine Mansfield" in *Virginia Woolf: A Feminist Slant* edited by Jane Marcus. Lincoln: University of Nebraska Press, 1983, p. 152-161.

Magalaner, Marvin. *The Fiction of Katherine Mansfield.* Carbondale, Southern Illinois University Press, 1971.

Mansfield, Katherine. *The Aloe, with Prelude,* edited with Introduction by Vincent O'Sullivan. Wellington: Port Nicholson Press, 1982.

———. *The Collected Letters of Katherine Mansfield.* Oxford: Clarendon Press, 1984 - V. 1: 1903-1917, V. 2: 1918-1919, V.3: 1919-1920, V.4: 1920-1921.

———. *Critical Writings,* edited and introduction by Clare Hanson. New York: St. Martin's Press, 1987.

———. *The Garden Party: Katherine Mansfield's New Zealand Stories,* illustrated edition. New York: New Amsterdam, 1988.

————. *Journal*, edited by John Middleton Murry, definitive edition. London: Constable, 1954.

————. *Letters*, edited by John Middleton Murry, special one volume edition. New York: Knopf, 1932.

————. *Letters Between Katherine Mansfield and John Middleton Murry*, edited by Cherry Hankin. London: Virago, 1988.

————. *Letters to John Middleton Murry, 1913-1922*, edited by John Middleton Murry. New York: Knopf , 1951.

————. *Novels and Novelists*, edited by John Middleton Murry, New York: Knopf, 1930.

————. *Poems of Katherine Mansfield*. Auckland: Oxford University Press, 1988.

————. *Scrapbook*, edited by John Middleton Murry, New York: Knopf, 1940.

————. *Short Stories*. New York: Knopf, 1941.

————. *Stories*, selected and with an introduction by Elizabeth Bowen. New York: Vintage, 1956.

————. *Stories of Katherine Mansfield,* Definitive Edition edited by Antony Alpers. Auckland: Oxford University Press, 1984.

————. *Undiscovered Country: The New Zealand Stories of Katherine Mansfield,* edited by Ian A. Gordon. London: Longman, 1974.

————. "Unpublished Manuscripts," transcribed and edited by Margaret Scott in *Turnbull Library Record,* NS; Vol. III, 1, March 1970, 4-28; Vol. III, 3, November 1970, 128-136; Vol. IV, 1, May 1971, 4-20; Vol. V, 1, May 1972, 19-25; Vol. III, 1, March 1970, 4-28; Vol. VI, 2, October 1973, 4-8; Vol. VII, 1, May 1974, 4-14.

————. *The Urewara Notebook*, edited with introduction by Ian A. Gordon. Wellington: Oxford University Press, 1978.

Mantz, Ruth Elvish. *Critical Bibliography of Katherine Mansfield.* London: Constable, 1931.

————, and John Middleton Murry. *The Life of Katherine Mansfield.* London: Constable, 1933.

Merlin, Roland. *Le Drame Secret de Katherine Mansfield.* Pierres Vives: 1950.

Merriam-Webster's Encyclopedia of Literature. Springfield: Merriam-Webster, 1995.

Meyers, Jeffery. *Katherine Mansfield: A Biography.* New York: New Directions, 1978.

Moers, Ellen. *Literary Women.* New York: Anchor, 1977.

Moorman, Lewis J. *Tuberculosis and Genius.* Chicago: University of Chicago Press, 1940.

Moran, Patricia. "Unholy Meanings: Maternity, Creativity, and Orality in Katherine Mansfield." *Feminist Studies* 17:1. Spring 1991: 105-125.

———. *Word of Mouth: Body Language in Katherine Mansfield and Virginia Woolf.* Charlottesville and London: University Press of Virginia, 1996.

Morrow, Patrick. "Katherine Mansfield and World War I" in *Literature and War,* edited by David Bevan. Amsterdam and Atlanta: Rodopi, 1990. p. 39-43.

Morrow, Patrick D. *Katherine Mansfield's Fiction* Bowling Green, OH: Bowling Green State University Popular Press, 1993.

Murray, Heather. *Double Lives: Women in the Stories of Katherine Mansfield.* Dunedin, N.Z.: University of Otago Press, 1990.

Murry, John Middleton. *Between Two Worlds, An Autobiography.* London: Jonathan Cape, 1935.

———. "The Isolation of Katherine Mansfield" in *The Adelphi,* XXIII (January-March 1947), 49-54.

———. "Katherine Mansfield in France" in *Atlantic,* CLXXXIV (September 1949), 278-284.

———. *Katherine Mansfield and Other Literary Portraits.* New York: British Book Center, 1950.

Nathan, Rhoda B. ed. *Critical Essays of Katherine Mansfield.* New York: G.K. Hall; Toronto: Maxwell Macmillan Canada; New York: Maxwell Macmillan International, 1993.

———. *Katherine Mansfield.* New York: Continuum, 1988.

Norman, Sylvia. "A World on Katherine Mansfield" in *Fortnightly Review,* CLXIX (April 1948), 278-284.

O'Sullivan, Vincent. "Finding the Pattern, Solving the Problem: Katherine Mansfield the New Zealand European" in *Katherine Mansfield: In From the Margin,* edited by Roger Robinson. Baton Rouge and London: Louisiana State University Press, 1994. p. 9-24.

Pilditch, Jan, ed. *The Critical Response to Katherine Mansfield.* (Critical Responses in Arts and Letters, Number 21). Westport, CT and London: Greenwood Press, 1996.

Porter, Katherine Ann. "The Art of Katherine Mansfield" in *The Days Before.* New York: Harcout Brace, 1952, pp. 82-87.

Pratt, Susan L. *Reading the Feminine in the Major Stories of Katherine Mansfield.* Ann Arbor: University Microfilms International, 1992.

Pritchett, V. S. "Minor Masterpieces" in *New Statesman and Nation,* XXXI (February 2, 1946), 87.

Rich, Adrienne Cecile. *Of Woman Born: Motherhood as Experience and Institution.* New York: Norton, 1976.

Robinson, Roger, ed. *Katherine Mansfield: In From the Margin.* Baton Rouge: Louisiana State University Press, 1994.

Scott, Margaret, "The Extant Manuscripts of Katherine Mansfield" in *Etudes Anglaises* XXVI (1973) 413-419. Also published in *The Critical Response to Katherine Mansfield*, edited by Jan Pilditch, Westport, CT and London: Greenwood Press, 1996. p. 113-119.

Showalter, Elaine. *A Literature of Their Own: British Women Novelists from Brontë to Lessing*. Princeton: Princeton University Press, 1977.

Swinnerton, Frank. *Background with Chorus*. London: Hutchinson, 1956.

Texas. University at Austin. Humanities Research Center. Katherine Mansfield: An Exhibition, September–November, 1973. Austin: The Center, 1975.

Tindall, William York. *Forces in Modern British Literature, 1885-1956*. New York, Vintage Books, 1956.

Thorp, Willard. "The Unburned Letters of Katherine Mansfield" in *New Republic*, CXXVI (January 7, 1952), 18.

Tomalin, Claire. *Katherine Mansfield: A Secret Life*. New York: Knopf, 1988.

Tytler, Graeme. "Mansfield's 'The Voyage'" in *The Explicator,* 50: (Fall 1991): 42-45

Wagenknecht, Edward. Review of *Scrapbook* in *New York Times Book Review* (February 11, 1940), 2.

Waldron, Philip. "Katherine Mansfield's Journal" in *Twentieth Century Literature: A Scholarly and Critical Journal*. 20 (1974): 11-18.

West, Jessamyn. "In Search of Purity" in *Saturday Review*, XL (September 21, 1957), 13.

Whitridge, Arnold. "Katherine Mansfield" in *Sewanee Review*, XLVIII (April 1940), 256-272.

Wright, Celeste T. "Darkness as a Symbol in Katherine Mansfield" in *Modern Philology*, LI (February 1954), 204-207.

———. "Genesis of a Story" in Philological Quarterly, XXIV (January 1955), 91-96.

———. "Katherine Mansfield's Boat Image" in *Twentieth Century Literature*, I (October 1955), 123-132.

———. "Katherine Mansfield's Secret Smile" in *Literature and Psychology*, V (August 1955), 44-48.

Index

About the Author

KATHERINE MURPHY DICKSON is Reference Librarian at the Nimitz Library, United States Naval Academy, Annapolis Maryland. She earned a bachelor's degree in library science from Simmons College, a master's degree in modern British literature from Columbia University, and a doctorate in American Studies/Women's Studies from the University of Maryland. She is the author of *Sexism and Reentry: Job Realities for Women Librarians*.